KU-300-067

GOD IN THE GALLERY

Donald English

GOD
IN THE
GALLERY

London EPWORTH PRESS

© Donald English
First published 1975
by Epworth Press
All rights reserved

No part of this publication may be
reproduced, stored in a
retrieval system, or
transmitted, in any form or by
any means, electronic, mechanical,
photocopying, recording or
otherwise, without the prior
permission of Epworth Press

7162 0245 x

Enquiries should be addressed to
The Methodist Publishing House
Wellington Road
Wimbledon
London SW19 8EU
Printed in Great Britain by
Ebenezer Baylis & Son Ltd
The Trinity Press
Worcester, and London

Contents

Contents

For Bertha

For Barbara

Preface

THIS is a book for those who wish their worship to be more meaningful and true. It does not offer blueprints or liturgies: it is basically about those attitudes out of which worship grows, about the presuppositions which inform the content and determine the orders of worship. It is therefore an invitation to readers to share an exploration behind and beneath the worship we offer. The questions and work suggested at the end of the chapters are meant to extend the exploration beyond the confines of this book, both for individuals and groups.

The material began life as lectures and talks to ministers and local preachers, some of whom were kind enough to suggest publication. The Rev. John Stacey, the Chairman of the Editional Sub-committee of Epworth Press, generously made this possible and has patiently awaited the final manuscript and made most helpful suggestions meanwhile, though his responsibility for the contents ends at that point.

Mrs Joan Roebuck typed some of the final manuscript; I am grateful for her help, as I am to Bertha, my wife, who typed the rest, as well as giving constant encouragement. Finally, I am thankful for all those, Methodists and others, with whom I have had the privilege of worshipping over the years, and whose fellowship inspires one to be concerned to offer the very best in our service of God.

DONALD ENGLISH

Introduction

'CHRISTIAN worship is the most momentous, the most urgent, the most glorious action that can take place in human life.' So wrote the late Karl Barth.[1] What an exciting prospect that definition opens up for the would-be worshipper. But what is the reality to which he will be introduced on his first day at church? The minister/priest/preacher enters. There is some kind of call to worship. What thoughts pass through the minds of the worshippers at this point? 'The minister looks well/ill/fresh/tired this morning. I see Mrs X is/isn't here. Why does the service begin in the same/in a different way each week? I hope the first hymn will be soft/loud/peaceful/rousing/long/short. It's very warm/cold/clear/stuffy in here today. And finally, did I switch the gas on/off? And so on. The adjectives 'momentous', 'urgent' and 'glorious' are hardly those which come most readily to mind as an accurate description of such thoughts. If God is present at all in such thoughts He has at least been relegated to the gallery.

The fact seems to be that our Christian description of worship at its best, and our Christian experience of worship as we currently know it, are rather far removed one from the other. The purpose of this book is to examine the causes of such separation and to suggest and explore one way—perhaps the most important way—of bridging the gap. We shall indicate this by means of a number of comments on worship from different writers.

The first comes from what is at first, perhaps, an unlikely starting point; an article in the Arts column of the *Guardian*. In January 1972, the Welsh Arts Council organized an exhibition on 'Worship' at Bolton Art Gallery. The *Guardian* reviewer was Merete Bates, who commented, 'In balance, the exhibition has

[1] Quoted in J. J. von Allmen, *Worship: Its Theology and Practice*, Lutterworth 1965, p. 13.

a slightly maudlin, obsessive, guilty sense about it. More worship of death than life. This need not have happened if the organisers had not so closely identified "Worship" with religion.' Bates went on to argue that aspects of experience like common love should also be included in such an exhibition. We need not go into that discussion here. What emerges from this review, however, is that *one's understanding of what worship is* will greatly influence both one's attitude to it and the contents one wishes to include in it. If, for example, one sees worship in the traditional religious terms of awareness of God, then one's expectations of worship, and the actual contents of worship will be determined by this consideration. However, if one views worship as an exploration of the human spirit, and of those experiences in life which draw us out of our selfishness into concern for and action towards others, then a different expectation and content are called for.[2] In the following pages, therefore, we shall try to clarify our understanding of the nature of worship.

To do so, however, we must face the fact that we cannot satisfactorily define worship as an isolated entity; as *something we do*. Martin Achard points us in the right direction with his comment, 'It is generally admitted that the purpose of worship is to establish and, by means of its symbols and rites, to give expression to a relationship between man and the Godhead.[3] All readers may not wish to support every part of such a definition, and we do not wish to debate it here. What such a comment does help us to see, however, is that worship has to do with *a relationship*. At its heart lies the conviction that there is a God who can be known, to whom human beings can relate. It therefore follows that any deepening of our understanding of worship will be dependent upon a *deepening of our understanding of that relationship which worship is meant both to express and strengthen.* It is as we see more what we mean by a relationship with the Godhead that we shall understand worship better. This in turn means that the more we know about God and the more we

---

[2] Most books on worship offer a definition. For a recent attempt, based on a brief summary of biblical evidence, see the article 'Worship: its nature and function' by Michael Townsend, in *Worship and Preaching* Volume 4, No. 4, August 1974, p. 2. For suggestions concerning the main sections of worship, see *In Church*, ed. John Stacey, L.P. Dept. 1971, Chapters 1 and 4.

[3] See J. J. von Allmen (ed.), *Vocabulary of the Bible*, Lutterworth 1958, p. 471.

know about ourselves and our setting in relation to God, the better we shall understand and participate in worship.

The introduction of the word, 'setting' into the last sentence moves us on a little further. To deepen our understanding of worship we must explore more fully not only what we mean by a relationship with God, but also what we see as the relationship between worship and life as a whole. This is not to introduce at this point the somewhat overworked concept of 'relevance' in relation to worship. As Craddock has said, 'A premature or hasty demand for relevance paralyses thought which could, in the larger perspective, prove to be the most relevant after all'.[4] Rather we are seeking here to ask whether worship is limited to certain acts, times and places, or whether the relationship it expresses is a true basis for the whole of life. Again we may turn to Martin Achard: 'It is significant that Hebrew has one word to denote work, service and worship; in biblical thought there is no watertight division between daily work and the adoration of God; in the very first pages of the Scripture manual activity and the service of the Creator are inseparably linked. The cult, in the narrow sense in which we understand it today, forms part of a vast service which God expects of His people, or better still, everything which the believers do can and ought to be an act of worship, carried out for the honour of God.'[5] Our task is therefore greater than the examination of our relationship to God and our understanding of those involved in such a relationship; it extends to a sympathetic sense of what is going on in the world, and of how worship has a place in what is going on. In short, the basis of a deepening worship is a deepening sense of the religious understanding of life as a whole. As we see the whole of life as lived in some relationship to God our acts of worship may express that relationship, and do so more meaningfully.

Thus we are really committed to an examination of our presuppositions in worship; 'our' meaning both individual worshippers and the Church as a whole. This differs from many modern approaches in two ways. In the first place, so much modern thought about worship goes into 'preparing things for

[4] F. B. Craddock, *The Pre-existence of Christ in the New Testament*, Abingdon Press 1968, p. 108f.
[5] *Vocabulary of the Bible*, p. 472.

the congregation'. Experts (and non-experts) seek to introduce new forms of worship, new shapes of liturgy, new types of music, new expressions of modern Christian outlooks, new thought-forms more fitted to modern men, new arrangements of the seating, the communion table position, or the place of the pulpit. All of this is undoubtedly necessary work; without it we so easily fall into a semi-comatose state by reason of the familiarity with which we follow well-worn paths. But their weakness is that they all seem to involve the congregation in 'waiting for the next form of service'. The people in the pew are in danger of becoming connoisseurs of liturgical form (and mal-form): or patient sufferers of the results of other people's bright ideas. The responsibility for the failure of worship to excite us, and for the provision of the remedy, evidently lies with 'them', the professionals, not with 'us' the congregation. A subtle danger here is that a premium is put on services which 'excite', 'grip', 'thrill', rather than upon those which are 'true' and 'meaningful'. Of course they may be both, but the experimenter soon discovers the pressures for the former rather than the latter. Each one must offer 'more' than the previous service.[6] The purpose of this book is to ask members of congregations (as well as compilers of new forms of worship), whether the fault and the responsibility do not in fact lie with their wrong presuppositions about the basis of worship, or at least with the insufficient attention that is paid to such presuppositions. It is a sobering fact of history that in times of revival the Church is rarely troubled about the shape of her liturgy. People are in the right spirit; they have their sense of values right, and the worship lives. Of course forms used in times of revival will not always sustain the Church during other times and phases in her life. But there is, at such times, in general a satisfying meaningfulness and a spontaneous creativity which

---

[6] As an illustration of this point see John Killinger, *Leave it to the Spirit*, S.C.M. 1971, p. 5, where a 'Scapegoat Service' is described. People disrobe, write on one another's bodies with grease crayon, attack a man standing on the altar dressed in white. Then words from Isaiah 53 are read. The author admits this is probably too daring, but suggests it is what we should be doing, at least occasionally, first because modern cultural expressions are like that—'everything is allowed' (p. 10)— and second, because we need to 'respond to the wildness of God' (p. 11). The point here is not, 'How could we keep that sort of thing up, and who would come?', but are modern artistic forms of expression necessarily valid norms for our worship and is it accurate theologically to speak of 'the wildness of God?'

are often lacking at other times. The point here is not to 'start a revival'—properly a contradiction in terms—but rather to draw attention to those characteristics of worship which are evident at times when the Church's devotion has been intense and her effectiveness great. Our modern worship may not be put right by new forms but by a new spirit of conviction, a new understanding of the basis of worship, a new concern that our basic beliefs should directly influence our services. This means *placing the responsibility upon the total Church.*

In the second place this approach differs from many modern approaches in the way in which a *recipe book* differs from a book on *marriage guidance.* The recipe book contains lists of ingredients. If the dish is not immediately successful then one adds a little more of one commodity, a little less of another. After a while, with ingredients well balanced to taste, one ends up with the right mixture. The onlooker can hardly be blamed for thinking that this is the approach to much modern worship. With the increase of ecumenical work and awareness, each denomination is learning forms of worship from each other.[7] Special orders are produced for special occasions, so that we may all take part with a clear conscience and a sense that somewhere in the service there is, 'a bit of ours'. Denominational liturgies also increasingly contain sections, orders, or styles which are borrowed from outside their own tradition. Now it can hardly be doubted that such sharing and awareness of others can help us all (though this is not as inevitable as we are sometimes led to think). But the danger of the 'recipe mentality' is very great. For it can externalize worship, producing new forms to follow, without leading us to the heart of the problem in our own condition. Perhaps we need to read again the words of William Law: 'For the Son of God did not come from above to add an external form of worship to the several ways of life that are in the world, and so leave people to live as they did before, in such tempers and enjoyments as the spirit and fashion of the world approves; but ... to call mankind to a divine and heavenly life; to the highest change of their own nature and temper, to be born again of the Holy Spirit; to walk in the

[7] For a writer who notes this as one of the encouraging signs in the ecumenical situation see David L. Edwards's Introduction (pp. 7–8) in Peter Morgan (ed.), *Unity: The Next Step*, S.P.C.K. 1972.

wisdom and light and love of God, and to be like Him to the utmost of their power. . . .'[8] Of course, as we shall assert more strongly later, our forms of service are meant to influence us in this direction, and those who formulate new services have this in mind. A properly prepared liturgy will both enable the worshipper to express his worship and introduce him to those aspects of worship which he might otherwise neglect. There can, therefore, be a direct and proper link between the outward form of the liturgy and the inner condition of the worshipper. The extent to which this link depends upon proper instruction both in the contents of the faith *and* in the art of using a formal liturgy does not yet appear to have been apprehended by denominations without such a tradition. Those denominations with liturgical traditions normally use confirmation training to teach this art. For those not so taught a new liturgy may easily fail to be a mode of expression or edification in worship. The recipe mentality is thus prevalent more amongst those who are presented with the orders than amongst those who create them. It is timely, therefore, for us to be called again to see that there is another side to our approach to worship; the side which looks not so much at outward forms but at inner condition.

This is where the marriage guidance approach comes in. A marriage guidance counsellor who helped people by handing out a list of recipes for happy marriages would not last long in the job. Life, he would be told (and especially married life), is too complex and rich to be trivialized by that kind of simplistic approach. The best advice for marriage is contained, not in little lists of 'dos and don'ts', but in an understanding of the basic principles on which successful marriage is based. These include an insight into what marriage is about; oneness of two people, sharing and caring; sympathy, gentleness, tolerance; love and loyalty. These are not recipes; they are descriptions of the various forces of the dynamism of life. One can control the ingredients of a recipe; one is controlled by the attitudes listed above. Two ounces of lard remain two ounces of lard however you view them: there is no telling what a little bit of genuine love will become.

So here we are trying to ask ourselves about the proper

[8] *A Serious Call to a Devout and Holy Life*, Fontana Paperback 1965, p. 95.

understanding, insights and attitudes on which true worship is based. We do this in no sense to the detriment of modern concerns with form and experiment. But we do it to correct the balance; to guard against the tendency to replace unsatisfactory fruit with artificial fruit tied on to the branches. We wish to ask about the root of our worship. Perhaps some words of Beckmann, quoted by J. J. von Allmen, will indicate the spirit of our approach. 'Christian worship is, in essence, not a theological blueprint drawn up by specialists, but an event, an encounter between the Lord, who through the Holy Spirit acts in Word and Sacrament, and His people; its liturgical form is the fruit of faith and experience.'[9] It is on that faith and experience that we shall concentrate our attention, for its failure may be the cause of the apparent weakness of much of our worship.

We shall not be attempting to establish a set of qualifications without which true worship cannot be offered, a kind of religious means-test. The whole concept of qualification is made absurd by the biblical concept of grace. But we are insisting that worship depends upon the existence of a certain relationship between the worshipper and God. We are also seeking to show that our presuppositions inform our worship; and that our worship ought to deepen our presuppositions. As Evelyn Underhill put it, 'the character of worship is always decided by the worshipper's conception of God and his relation to God: that is to say, whatever its ritual expression may be, it always has a theological basis'.[10]

We may list the presuppositions, as a guide to the reader, in the form of the following simple sentences: *God is, through Jesus Christ, by the Holy Spirit. I am, with them, around the Bible, with the Sacraments, in the world, now.* Each chapter expounds one of these statements, then offers questions for discussion and practical suggestions for the outworking of discussion in acts of worship.

---

[9] *Worship: Its Theology and Practice*, p. 13.
[10] *Worship*, Nisbett 1941, p. 60.

Chapter One

GOD IS

THE writer of the Letter to the Hebrews asserts that, 'whoever would draw near to God must believe that he exists' (Heb. 11:6). The being of God is both the basic condition and the ultimate object of our worship. It is surely no coincidence that the age which has had such doubts about His existence is also the age which has seen such a decline in the quality and attractiveness of its worship.

It is equally clear that an age which lacks certainty about God will soon lack fervour and conviction. The cry for good modern hymns is often a vain cry for that reason. Hymnology usually reflects the spiritual condition of the times. (Charles Wesley's hymns are an obvious example.) Most modern religious songs of worth, however, seem to be satirical comments on Christian thinking and action or commendatory accounts of man helping man. Witness the moving comments by Gordon Wakefield in his final editorial for *Worship and Preaching* (Vol. 2, No. 6, p. 3). 'One of the ironies of my life is that just as the Churches as a whole were beginning to understand liturgy, the whole concept of the transcendent began to be questioned, so that those of us who were winning the battle for greater reverence and order in Church were suddenly taken in the rear by a large host, led by many former high churchmen, whose slogans were "relevance" and "humanity". Participation, intelligibility and experiment were the desiderata, and it seemed to be more important to go to Church to meet your neighbour than to meet God. Psychology replaced theology and the end of worship was not to be made prostrate before the ineffable wonder of the Divine Grace but to clothe the naked, feed the hungry, and secure justice on earth.' This provocative testimony provides an interesting historical comment on recent developments in worship. One simply wishes to respond by suggesting that theology has in fact been replaced, not by the

narrower field of psychology, but by the wider one of anthropology, if one may include within its sphere the various
behavioural sciences.

In arguing for the place of such songs in our modern worship,
Douglas Galbraith rightly comments, 'Now no one is suggesting
that this kind of thing is hymnody. Hymns are other directed
and point away from the worshippers; these songs indulge in
self-examination.'[1] Our difficulty is that while there may be
place for this kind of song in our services, we know very well
that our total diet of worship cannot be sustained by them. If
they are songs trying to ask relevant and difficult and agonizing
questions, then they may only be used against the background
of something to be questioned. Galbraith also quotes Geddes
Macgregor's comment that, 'Christianity is big with doubt, but
the doubt never catches up with the faith'. One wonders how
true an assessment that is of the modern output of hymns and
songs. What we lack is sufficient affirmation to provide the
content for questioning. And that lack comes from our uncertainty about the object of our worship, God Himself. The
same is true about the lifelessness and unexpectancy of much of
our public prayer; the unenthusiastic reading of and listening
to the Bible, the unease about the value of the sermon. Once the
being of God is in doubt it is natural that the whole structure of
worship is threatened.

Now plainly one cannot simply ask that since such doubt
threatens our worship then we must ban doubt! ('If I were going
to Cambridge I wouldn't be starting from here.') The underlying causes of doubt concerning the existence of God, and of
the Christian religion as a whole, have been as carefully
expressed and documented by Christians as by anyone else; a
fact which is not without its own significance when concern for
the truth is under debate. *Religion and Change* by David L.
Edwards (S.C.M. 1969) is a useful case in point. When other
disciplines make claims to insights into truth which challenge
Christian affirmations, then the Christian cannot simply
ignore such claims and hope that they (or those who make
them) will go away. To do so may well be to miss the road to
deeper Christian insights into truth. If Christianity is true, then

[1] *Square Dance in Heaven: Words and Music in the Worship of the Church Today* (Iona
Community pamphlet), p. 6.

the Christian has nothing to fear from truth which is disclosed to him from any source, even if it undermines that which he previously held to be part of the Christian understanding of truth.

Nevertheless, certain qualifying comments are probably fitting at this point, particularly concerning Christian responses to new knowledge gained and new claims made from other disciplines such as the behavioural sciences, and also to the general intellectual and scientific ethos within which most of our thinking is done in the late twentieth century and in our Western culture.

The first is that responses which involve denial of traditionally held Christian doctrines often receive attention out of all proportion to their ultimate value. The recent 'Death of God' controversy may prove to be a good illustration. Such developments are suddenly 'news' and receive maximum coverage from the communication media. But such sudden and total exposure is not always conducive to a careful exposition, understanding and application of the new position adopted. Receiving this impetus to unnaturally speedy growth it is forced to spread beyond the proper height its rootage permits. A genuine awareness is forced to service what becomes a 'ten-day wonder' and is unable to sustain its impact, or to become a permanent element undergirding Christian worship.

Secondly, and arising from the above, this maximum coverage by the media produces diluted, exaggerated or otherwise distorted versions of the position adumbrated, so that many—including Christians—who depend upon the media for their information receive an unclear impression of what the issues are. What they do gather, however, is that some aspect of traditional Christian belief is now being questioned or jettisoned by some Christian thinkers or leaders. Thus, without being able to understand the real problem, and without being trained sufficiently to read the new books themselves, they have a question mark placed against some part, or the whole, of their faith, and may find themselves unable to deal with it. Worship goes on for them, but the cumulative effect of the question marks now established can be disastrous in relation to the meaningfulness of worship. The difficulty is not that questions have been raised about the faith. It is that they have been raised in a way with which the ordinary believer finds it difficult to cope.

In the third place he may not be too clear about the basic Christian dogma which is under attack and may well lose something vital to his faith as a result. If, for example, the nearest he has come to understanding God's transcendence has been to see it in wholly spatial terms, with God 'out there' occupying some unspecified space in the universe, then he may soon lose such a concept under the pressures of modern science and of Christian thinkers who respond positively to such pressures. But if the spatial model was the only one he possessed for belief in God's transcendence, he may now feel obliged to disbelieve in transcendence altogether. The effect of publicity about some new line of Christian thought has not been simply to destroy an inadequate model, but to discard the reality[2] altogether, a reality he was previously aware of, however inadequately. One does not pass any judgement on this process, since it could be argued that with such an inadequate model he would be better off starting all over again. One simply notes this element as one of those which has placed a severe question mark at the heart of worship for some people, without providing a way to face its implications.

Fourthly, however, and more hopefully, there have been two further developments as a result of twentieth-century challenges to Christianity (and the reality of God's existence in particular), and also as a result in part of those responses from Christians which seemed to other Christians to capitulate too easily in face of such challenges. For the sake of clarity, though as we shall see the division is too clear-cut, we may describe them as responses from the fields of revealed and natural theology; or as representing deductive and inductive processes. The former is largely biblically based, and seeks to understand, explain and apply that which is revealed in Scripture, and to do so in a way appropriate to the twentieth century. It is deductive in that it proceeds from revealed truth and deduces the implications and applications. The latter is based upon life as we now experience it, and asks questions about the meaning of that life, and of specific experiences. It is inductive in that it proceeds from this

[2] Assuming, for the moment, that it is valid to speak of God as 'transcendent'.

variety of questions to build up a case for the existence of 'otherness' in life, and of 'ultimate otherness', 'personal ultimate otherness', called God, without whom not only particular experiences but life as a whole is not properly understood or fully enjoyed.

Typical of the former approach is that of A. M. Ramsey in *God, Christ and the World* (S.C.M. 1969). Having disposed of the idea that transcendence inevitably involves a spatial model, and having shown that its basic meaning has always been 'otherness' he goes on, 'The truth of God's transcendence still stands. God is near, but God is different. God is here, but man is dependent. God's otherness is the otherness of Creator to creature, of Saviour to sinner; and it is for the creature still to worship the Creator and for the sinner still to ask for the Saviour's grace. Without this the new Christianity of the secular city will lose its identity as Christianity and will deceive itself and mislead its citizens. And, on the other hand, those who cherish God's transcendence will know that it is within the secular city that it has to be vindicated and that the transcendent and the numinous are to be seen not in a separated realm of religious practice but in human lives marked by an awe-inspiring self-forgetfulness, compassion, humility and courage' (pp. 29–30). This passage reveals certain characteristics of the modern deductive revelational approach. The norm for judgement of trust about God is that which He has revealed, supremely in the Bible (see the Creator—creature, Saviour—sinner, transcendence—nearness, patterns). And this kind of construction of our understanding of God must be witnessed to by the quality of human lives in which God reveals Himself (awe-inspiring, self-forgetfulness, compassion, humility and courage). But any claim for teaching and practice to be Christian must be tested by the norms of God's revelation of Himself in relation to the world (otherwise it will 'lose its identity as Christianity and will deceive itself and mislead its citizens').

One would wish to argue that John V. Taylor's *Go-Between God* (S.C.M. 1972) has the same approach at its centre, though with a very much greater concentration upon the realities of everyday life—especially personal relationships—as providing the materials for the awareness and disclosure of God the Holy Spirit. Here too the norms for identifying the awareness and the

disclosure are derived from the biblical record of God's revelation in Christ. Thus, after outlining three signs of the Holy
Spirit's creative activity in the world—the urge towards higher
consciousness and personhood, the occasion for spontaneity and
the necessity for choice, the principle of sacrifice and existence
for the other—he goes on, 'And, in the fulness of time, all of this
was perfectly disclosed in Jesus Christ, who was conceived by
the Holy Spirit and to whom the Holy Spirit has been directing
men ever since. It is not difficult to see how this must affect our
understanding of that mission which is the continuing Christ-
centred activity of that same Holy Spirit' (p. 36).

The inductive approach, more akin to natural theology than
revelational, is typified by Peter L. Berger in his book, *A Rumour
of Angels* (Pelican 1971). His approach is 'a spirit of patient
induction and an attitude of openness to the fullness of human
experience, especially as this experience is accessible to historical inquiry' (p. 104). Noting that we live in an age of the
'alleged demise of the supernatural' (p. 35) he reminds us of the
dictum of Dean Inge, 'a man who marries the spirit of the age
very soon finds himself a widower' (p. 37). However, as a matter
of observation he discovers that, 'For whatever reasons, sizeable
numbers of the specimen modern man have not lost a propensity for awe, for the uncanny, for all those possibilities that are
legislated against by the canons of secularized rationality'
(p. 39). We have a clear view of his basic method in the
conclusion that, 'the theological decision will have to be that,
"in, with and under" the immense array of human projections,
there are indicators of a reality that is truly "other", and that
the religious imagination of man ultimately reflects' (p. 65).
The search is for 'signals of transcendence' via 'prototypical
gestures' (p. 70), that is, pointers beyond natural reality,
arising from reiterated acts and experiences which express
essential elements of man's being. He finds such signals in man's
propensity for order, in his ability to play, in his quality of
hope, in the concept of damnation and in his capability of
humour. From the standpoint of such signals the characteristic
of our age may well be seen to be the shrinkage of the scope of
human experience. 'The denial of metaphysics may here be
identified with the triumph of triviality' (p. 96).

These two approaches—and the books quoted do not exhaust

the two methods by any means—are perhaps not to be placed too firmly as rivals. The former conclusions must be seen to work out in everyday life of man and to give a proper interpretation to the whole of life. The conclusions of the latter approach will need verification from somewhere if they are to be acknowledged as christian: it is difficult to believe that the biblical revelation in the tradition of the Church will not be the source of that verification. Yet their starting points *are* different, and the source of the authority of each needs to be carefully distinguished.

The overall point of interest for us, however, is that both from the revelational and natural theological position, from the deductive and inductive method, from the conservative and liberal outlook, there are signs of renewed awareness of the reality of God.

In the remainder of this chapter we explore three ways in which our beliefs about God have an important effect on our worship. These beliefs are characteristic of the traditional interpretations of biblical material; because this represents the author's standpoint. The link between belief and worship, however, may serve as a useful method also for those who do not state their ideas about God in this way.[3]

First, *the being of God gives worship its proper dimensions.* One of the greatest dangers in Christian worship is the narrowing of our perspectives by undue concentration upon a select few doctrinal insights or, still worse, upon certain aspects of life in the modern world. A proper understanding of the being of God will always serve as a corrective to this error.[4] Take, for example, the traditional Christian way of describing God as Transcendent and Immanent. A true understanding of what these mean will prevent our worship from becoming locked within the four walls of our worship centres, or within the stifling atmosphere created by our favourite thoughts about God.

To say that God is transcendent is not to place Him, spatially, 'out there', or 'up there'. Neither is it to assert that we must address Him at some fixed point in a building which, by reason of artistic, musical, architectural or ceremonial

---

[3] One makes this comment without offering evaluation of such ideas.

[4] See p. 24 for Berger's comment about shrinkage of the scope of human experience. This danger is equally present in Christian worship.

means has been invested with a numinous quality. To say that God is transcendent is to say that He is *other than we are*, as Archbishop Michael Ramsey has pointed out.[5] It is to say that He is neither locked up in His universe (nor in any part of it), nor limited to it or any part of it. Words like omniscient, omnipotent, omnipresent—beloved of theologians and hymn writers of earlier days—were attempts to give verbal shape to this concept of God's otherness, but in terms which people *did* understand; knowledge, power and presence.

Whether we find such terms expressive of our understanding, or whether we prefer to think in terms of 'the numinous', or are more helped by talk of 'indicator experiences'[6] or 'disclosure situations'[7] of beauty, mystery, inwardness, depth; we shall find that our openness to this side of God's nature will influence our worship in three ways.

In the first place it means that we shall be ready for very ordinary (or extraordinary) words, actions and thoughts to be transcended as they become the vehicles of our understanding of God's being; of His communication of Himself to us. Thus words, actions, thought forms which have been previously familiar to us—which have perhaps already helped us in the past or been largely meaningless to us in the past—suddenly take on altogether new significance for us in our relationship to God and our understanding of Him. The transcendent God is revealed in the transcendent experience.

Secondly, openness to God's transcendence involves us in seeing that the very words, actions and thoughts we have spoken of above are invested with a meaning which is both prior to them and independent of them. God is what He is whether we personally have so experienced Him to be what He is. He is not made to be something because we experience Him to be like that. Certainly He cannot be what He is to us until He is revealed to us like that; but He must be what He is prior to being revealed to us as He is, otherwise He could not be so revealed. Our experience-centred approach needs the cor-

---

[5] See p. 23 above.

[6] David G. Deekes in *Doing Theology*, Local Preachers' Dept. of the Methodist Church 1972, ch. 2, pp. 33ff., 'Religious Experience'.

[7] Ian T. Ramsey, *Christian Empiricism*, Sheldon Press 1974, pp. 159ff., and *Models for Divine Activity*, S.C.M. 1973, ch. 1.

rective of this reminder. He is what He is whether we discover Him or not. He is transcendent.

While serving in Nigeria the writer was told a story which seemed to illustrate what is virtually incapable of illustration unless one has experienced it. A missionary in Ghana went early one morning to a bush village to conduct a communion service. He prepared the elements and awaited the arrival of the people; but something plainly had gone wrong, for nobody came. Having come so far, however, he proceeded with the service, though somewhat lonely and disappointed. When he came to the point of the service where he said the words, 'Therefore with Angels and Archangels, and with all the company of heaven, we laud and magnify Thy glorious Name', something happened which transformed, or better transcended, his experience of that service. The meaning of those words hit him with a totally new force. How could he be lonely and disappointed if those words meant what they said? The whole service took on new meaning. It was an experience of transcendence; because God is like that.

This illustration points to a third influence upon our worship, namely that it enables us to perceive the limited nature of all those elements in our lives which threaten to become absolute over us, and to imprison us. Whatever political institutions (especially the more totalitarian), or social structures (of Church or State), or the prevailing morality (or immorality) of our culture; even the demand of the whole ethos of our life in the present: all are declared to be transient, relative and limited when seen in the light of the transcendent God. They are placed within a frame of reference which cuts them down to size. They are placed under the judgement of a different standard of existence altogether. Part of the freedom of the people of God is the freedom to recognize the implications of His transcendence for their existence, in their worship to affirm it and in their lives to experience it. Governments may be powerful: they are not all-powerful. Social structures may exercise constraint: they need not imprison. Cultural atmosphere may be influential: it is not necessarily all-pervasive. For the Christian, that is. It is this kind of truth at which Jesus hints when He reminds Pilate, 'You would have no power over me unless it had been given you from above' (John 19:11), and, 'My kingship is not of this world; if my kingship were of this world, my servants would fight, that I might not be handed over to the Jews', but my kingship is not from this world' (John 18:36). We have it, too, in Paul's assertion on Mars Hill, 'The God who made the world and everything in it, being Lord of heaven and earth, does not live in shrines made by man, nor is he served by human hands, as though he needed anything since he himself gives to all men life and breath and everything. And he made from one every nation of men to live on all the face of the earth, having determined allotted periods and the boundaries of their habitation, that they should seek God . . .' (Acts 17:24-27). Then he reminded his highly cultured, philosophical audience that the materials with which they dealt, the whole pattern of historical and geographical data, and the conclusions based upon them, were not ends in themselves, but were meant to lead to perception of the One who is other than we are, and yet is the one through whom and in whom our existence is possible for (quoting from their own poetic literature) 'In him we live and move and have our being' (Acts 17:28). It was this, too, which enabled Paul to testify to the ability to bear up in the midst of extreme persecution and hardship. His secret is, '. . . we look not to the things that are seen but to the things that are unseen: for the things that are seen are transient, but the things that are unseen are eternal' (II Cor. 4:18).

Under the influence of these insights our worship of the transcendent God becomes the occasion for genuine realism about life as it is. We are not encouraged to run away from responsibilities, to ignore authorities, to blind ourselves to our cultural setting. We have no need to do so, because we can assess them realistically, recognize the limited nature of their rights over us, and seek by proper means to prevent them from usurping God's place in life, and so enable them to play their proper, limited, role in our life and that of our fellows. Neither, therefore, do we submit ourselves unreservedly to any of these influences upon us or demands upon us, for our ultimate allegiance is to the transcendent God.

We ought, therefore, to expect our worship to result in our seeing our work, our family, our relationships, our responsibilities and our problems in a right perspective. We may hope that we shall perceive how limited and relative they are, beside the absolute claims of God upon us (often made upon us in the very areas we are describing—our citizenship, our work, our family life and so on—but in such a way that clarifies even more the subservient role of each of these 'authorities' over us). Our worship is not primarily for our benefit but neither is it invalid, or even suspect, because it does us good. If it establishes, confirms and deepens the relationship of creatures to their Creator, of the redeemed to their Redeemer, we might even expect it to be an exhilarating, liberating and satisfying experience.

Yet we must at once refer to the other dimension of worship which is added by the Immanence of God. Other than we are He may be, apart from us He is not. We have rightly asserted that our words, deeds and thoughts have an ultimate meaning in a reality which is beyond them, so that our use of them does not *create* that reality. Nevertheless we must go on to assert that we can expect our meeting with God, our awareness of Him to take place precisely within the area and use of our words, actions and thoughts. The various parts of our worship neither create Him nor call Him up (or down), but we may expect His presence with us in them all the same. In His sovereign freedom He chooses so to meet His people. Our thoughts, actions and words do not constitute the truth, but we believe that He will use them to communicate and celebrate it.

The writer recalls an occasion when at the beginning of a Church Fellowship the President of the Young Wives Group, herself a comparatively young Christian, led the prayers. The words were somehow not the usual ones with which the preachers lead prayer. They were in a way more ordinary. And yet all of us present were very deeply aware of God's presence, and of the reality of the truth about God which was the basis of the prayer and its words.

We may refer back to Paul on Mars Hill to see how closely transcendence and immanence are held together in a fully orbed Christian awareness of God. Having affirmed how totally God transcends (as well as originates) human life, Paul can at once add that 'we live and move and have our being in Him'. It appears that transcendence and immanence are each required as a proper point of reference for the other. However much we wish to declare God's immanence, His presence in the world, we may never do so to the loss of this transcendence. As Craddock puts it, 'Without the overreaching (or permeating) presence of the Transcendent, created values cease to be regarded as created, relative values cease to be relative. Just as the lack of a doctrine of creation resulted in ancient man's divinization of the world, the lack of transcendence can result in the absolutizing of history with all its social and political structures. The secularization of the world with all its values begins to be lost as that secularity becomes antonomous.'[8] The result is that at best God becomes locked up in this universe: at worst He 'dies'. Theology becomes anthropology; human life loses any standard of reference outside itself. The danger here is that current experience becomes the absolute authority, and in so doing limits the vision of what can yet be achieved, and steadily strangles the questioning about and seeking after that which is beyond itself, the ultimate result is nihilism.[9]

In the same way, however, transcendence cannot be stressed at the expense of immanence. An exclusively transcendent God may be an interesting concept for a select group of trained humans to debate, but as such He is not impinging greatly upon human life, except perhaps in the 'smash and grab' mythology famous in certain cultures. And such a god becomes simply one being over against others, and as such a limited being. If the danger of over-immanentism is nihilism, the danger of over-transcendence is irrelevance.

We have therefore to assert the immanence of God, and to learn how to recognize His presence amongst us. The statement earlier, that the transcendent God makes Himself known precisely in our words, actions and symbols indicates the direction our thought must take. Worship becomes for us an exercise in discovering the transcendent God at the very heart of everyday living. This, after all, is what so many of the parables did. Jesus saw what everyone else saw—a sower, the weather, local customs. Yet He saw in and beyond them something more—the extravagant grace of God, the involvement of God in establishing His Kingdom against the powers of

[8] F. B. Craddock, *The Pre-existence of Christ in the New Testament*, Abingdon Press 1968, p. 185.
[9] Ibid., p. 186.

evil, the welcome awaiting any who turned to Him. Once this perception of the immanence of God in our daily lives is quickened in worship it begins to shed a light upon all the rest. This is surely part of what George Wade Robinson was trying to express when he wrote:

'Heaven above is softer blue,
  Earth around is sweeter green;
Something lives in every hue,
  Christless eyes have never seen:
Birds with gladder songs o'erflow,
  Flowers with deeper beauties shine,
Since I know, as now I know,
  I am His, and He is mine.'

(M.H.B. 443)

The important thing for us here is not simply that natural phenomena were enhanced because of his religious experience, but that the experience itself was of everlasting love, God's love. He can later write:

'Heaven and earth may fade and flee,
First-born light in gloom decline;
But, while God and I shall be,
I am His, and He is mine.'

(M.H.B. 443 v. 3)

It is the transcendent God who is recognized to be immanent in the world which is enhanced by the presence of His love within it.

The same link between God's presence in the world and the uniqueness of His love is seen in Richard Jones's hymn 'God of concrete, God of steel' (*Hymns and Songs* 23). The successive verses claim all the world of power, speed and truth for God, then follows:

'God whose glory fills the earth,
Gave the universe its birth
Loosed the Christ with Easter's might,
Saves the world from evil's blight,
Claims mankind by grace divine,
ALL THE WORLD OF LOVE IS THINE.'

Again it is God's transcendence—seen in giving birth to the universe and in divine grace, summed up in love—which gives the immanence of God's its characteristic recognition signs. Our worship of the immanent God should enable us to perceive His presence in our lives day by day.

It is as we become more aware, or aware again, or aware for the first time, of what it means to worship a God who is both transcendent and immanent that our worship will break free from its stifling narrowness and have truly wide dimensions, the dimensions of the being of God Himself.

The being of God provides worship with more than dimensions, however. *It also gives our worship its points of reference.* Points of reference are absolutely vital in so many walks of life. The writer recalls an experience during Royal Air Force officer training when another cadet was asked to teach the rest of the squad how to 'Right Dress'. He did everything to perfection except for one omission—he forgot to tell the marker, on whom everyone else in the line was focusing for position, to stand still. The result was that just as we all got into a straight line with the marker as our guide, he began to move forwards and backwards. The entire line followed and the squad swayed across the parade ground like a West Indian palm tree in the breeze! We were without a point of reference and the result was disastrous. The being of God provides points of reference for worship. He provides its centre of meaning, its authentication. Take, for example, the statement, 'God is Loving'. Understood in terms of the biblical concept of *agape*, the divine love which flows out and on in endless self-giving for the loved one, irrespective of deserving, this part of God's being becomes an anchor for our worship. It also provides a vantage point from which to view not only the saving acts which are part of the basis of our Christian life, but also the events of contemporary life, our own personal experiences, our attitudes to those who need our love, our need to be filled and motivated by that love.

Consideration of this point of reference will prevent us from becoming merely sentimental about God, life and people. It will reveal to us the utter hypocrisy involved in talking, singing, praying and preaching about love without doing anything in the world for those who need love. It will constantly bring us to our knees in the realization of how little of that kind of love is seen in our lives by others. And it will cause us to be more open to the influence of that love upon our own lives. Thus a point of reference becomes a point of renewal in worship.

An example of how this point is quickly lost, or easily missed, was the debate between what were called 'the evangelical gospel' and the 'social gospel'. Here a debate about priorities soon became a debate about alternatives. But the question, 'What is the nature of the love of God which is at the heart of the Christian gospel, and of which the Christian is seeking to be the instrument?' reveals how inadequate is either of the proposed answers on its own, for divine love will seek to meet every need of the loved one. The debate about priorities will continue: that about alternatives could be dropped.[10]

The same is true of the concept of God as Righteous. The three strands of biblical meaning here are that God is right, does right and puts people in the right. To have this as a point of reference is to look at our attitudes and actions in its light; it is to ask ourselves what kind of a world we live in and what the servants of a righteous God should be and do in such a world. It will be a healthy corrective to our easy-going tolerance, a stimulus to our concern for world justice; a reminder of our own short-comings, and a source of assurance that in a world that often defies moral explanation there is a God whose actions are righteous. Again the point of reference becomes a point of renewal.

Or we may say that God is Holy. Here is another point of reference for our worship. Isaiah's well-known vision of God in the temple, recorded in Isaiah 6, gives us some idea of the significance of this point of reference. To be aware of God's holiness is to glimpse His perfection, to feel the awesome presence of purity, to be grasped by that which is altogether clean. Such a realization should introduce a proper sense of reference so often lacking from our worship. It will also lead

---

[10] At the time of writing, the Lausanne Congress of the World Evangelical Alliance—a Congress primarily concerned with Evangelism—has recently met (July 1974) and has given a very significant place to social, political and economic problems without in any way undermining or detracting from the basic evangelical gospel or the importance of regeneration by the Holy Spirit of those who repent and believe the gospel. A forthcoming publication will contain the addresses and conclusions of the Congress.

2

to a sense of what sin really means, as it did for Isaiah: prayers
for forgiveness are never a mere formality for a congregation
which is aware of God's holiness. And it will add a focal point
for cleansing, a place in the service where we perceive and
reach out for the possibility of being made and kept clean
throughout our whole being and life. It is to breathe the purer
air of God's presence and be different. This is what Isaiah 6 is
about: it is meant to be a regular experience of the worshipping
community. But it needs the point of reference.

It is points of reference like this which hold worship together.
Anyone who has changed a car wheel will appreciate the
importance of the bolts which hold the wheel in place. They
secure the wheel so that it may properly perform its task; to
turn safely and effectively. The attributes of God we have been
considering provide this function for our worship. As we centre
our thought and worship upon them, our hymns and prayers,
our preaching and giving revolve securely and meaningfully
around the proper points of reference. The concepts of love,
righteousness, holiness—and others—are kept from vagueness
and shallowness. The character of God fills them with meaning.

In the third place, the being of God *gives direction to our
worship*. The danger of our reflections so far is that they could
lead to an endless round of contemplation of God and reflection
upon ourselves. But worship truly based upon the character of
God can never remain static and self-centred. It will have a
practical content and an active outworking.

Take, for example, the thought of God as Creator. The
Psalmist sets his worship against such a background, as in
Psalm 148. The directional effect of such a concept is enormous.
How can we begin worship without contemplating the immen-
sity of the universe and expressing our wonder and gratitude
about it to the One whose it is? And how can we ponder its
intention without coming to confess our part in the responsibility
for the sorry state it is now in? Millions of starving people in a
world with enough food potential for all; masses of people
living under-privileged lives for no other reason than that they
happened to be born in the wrong part of the world; millions
of illiterate adults in a world which has the most delicate and
powerful means of communication; the increasing fragmentation of life in a world which is increasingly aware of its oneness.

These things, by any standards, are foolish: in the presence of the Creator God they become blasphemous. Can we think about that in worship without feeling the need for confession and pardon? And how can worship of the Creator God fail to lead to action (I almost wrote 'erupt into action')? How can we survey the difference between God's plan for His world and its present condition without feeling the call to give ourselves in some measure to bridging the gap between the two? If we worship a God who is Creator we cannot expect to be left undisturbed or inactive. There is direction present.

In passing one wonders whether we are here at the source of the failure of the Christian Church to do as much for the under-privileged as she might. Compared with Christians in other ages we no doubt emerge well, but compared with our knowledge of the problems and the potential we possess the story is a very different one. It may be that the propaganda drawing attention to world need has succeeded only too well. By appealing to our natural human compassion it has helped to place the whole problem there—a human problem requiring human response. Thus Christians are by no means unique in seeking to help. But what difference does it make when I stop seeing the problem from the point of view of a fellow human being, and begin to sense how the Creator God feels about it? To accept the next step and acknowledge the call of that God to be fellow-workers in His creation, righting the blasphemy of under-privilege, injustice and man's inhumanity to man would surely not allow us to face the problems with the leisure at present characteristic of us. A friend of mine once sat outside a church waiting to collect a member of the congregation. The preacher went on with the service forty-five minutes beyond its normal finishing point. When at last the benediction was pronounced the doors of the church burst open and people scuttled out in all directions. One suspects that their main concern was for the fate of their Sunday joint! But perhaps most of our services *ought* to end with such urgent haste, in order that we might get out, not to rescue the lunch but to play our part in making the world what the Creator God intended it to be.

Direction of a different kind is possible, also. Often we come to worship obsessed by the problems we face; problems of family, work, relationships, illness, money, and a host of other elements which constitute everyday life. To worship the Creator God should provide some direction here, too; the direction of the light at the end of the tunnel. We may see this working out in Acts, chapter 4. Peter and John have been set free by the religious leaders, yet the Christian cause is still under strong threat. The reaction of the leaders is clearly reflected in Peter's prayer. 'Sovereign Lord, who didst make the heaven and the earth and the sea and everything in them . . .' (Acts 4:24— read Acts 3–4:22 for the setting). He then proceeds to rehearse past history and to present the problems of the moment. The point for us is that their first instinct was to place their problem in its proper perspective; against the background of a Creator God. If He can create a universe like ours, with its endless wonders, forces, and variety; a world which passes effortlessly from season to season, and through change after change, how can I treat this problem of mine as either a great one or an impossible one for Him? We so often come to worship tied up and imprisoned by the events, perplexities, problems of the past week. Such worship, in the presence of the Creator, can set us free from our prisons; free from the imagined enclosure of life; free to play our part in His world again. We leave with a new sense of direction when the perspective is restored and we see our problems in their correct proportions.

Or we may take the understanding of God as Redeemer. To redeem, in the biblical idiom, is to set someone free, at cost to oneself. In the New Testament it centres upon God setting us free at the cost of Christ's death for us. Paul expresses it well in Colossians 1, verses 12 to 14, '. . . giving thanks to the Father, who has qualified us to share in the inheritance of the saints in light. He has delivered us from the dominion of darkness and transferred us to the kingdom of his beloved Son, in whom we have redemption, the forgiveness of sins.' Worship can never be static with such an idea at its heart. We are able to offer worship only because we are 'the redeemed'; those who have been and are being delivered by God's grace. Worship is therefore a movement towards God, and of God towards us, that we may again experience the grace which He freely gives to us. It is a celebration of the freedom of the people of God; freedom from the forces which seek to pull us down morally, to enclose us socially, to isolate us personally. To be redeemed is to be set free, and our worship declares it. 'Sin will have no dominion over you,' writes Paul to the Romans (Rom. 6:14). One wonders how we manage to sit still for so long when our worship is celebrating a truth like that!

In such a setting worship truly becomes a celebration. It is good to be free and the people of God should enjoy their freedom together. But it is also a renewed invitation to explore the depths (or heights) of freedom available. As life develops all kinds of new freedoms—and rediscoveries of old ones—are possible. 'Static' Christianity becomes a contradiction in terms. Life is meant to involve progressive and ever-deepening experience of that one redemption in Jesus Christ. In worship, therefore, we not only celebrate—as at a birthday—but we also take stock of ourselves; also as at a birthday. Thus we not only joyfully explore the areas of freedom we have reached; we also seek to be open to new areas. The concept of growth can never be far away.

But this concept offers direction in another sense, too. If God is Redeemer for us, is He not also Redeemer of the whole world? But how can they enter into this redemption which we enjoy? As Paul knew, someone will have to tell them (Rom. 10:14). How can we truly worship the Redeemer God who, at great cost, has set us free, and not be deeply concerned for all those whom He longs to set free but who have not yet heard the news, or who have yet to see Christians sufficiently caring for them, or sufficiently reflecting Christ, to make the message convincing? To worship the Redeemer God Sunday by Sunday is to receive marching orders straight out into the world Sunday by Sunday, that all may have the opportunity to enter into the redemption won for them. One might add that those who in worship are truly entering into the experience of being liberated are more likely to wish others to be liberated also— and to do something about it. Do some of our failures in evangelism stem from the fact that we try to 'engage in' evangelism without properly 'thinking' evangelism? To partici-pate in an evangelistic activity is one thing, to be convinced about its purpose and necessity is another. But if our church members are not themselves entering more and more fully and joyfully into the experience of being redeemed it is not likely

that they will be convinced about the need to introduce others
to the experience of Christ in their lives. At the heart of genuine
evangelism there is the kind of testimony to the Jewish religious
leaders recorded of Peter in reply to the prohibition of further
evangelistic activity, 'We cannot but speak of what we have seen
and heard' (Acts 4:20). It is too much to expect that our acts of
worship will be one occasion when we 'see and hear' that which
inspires our verbal witness in daily life?

Then there is the understanding of God as Judge. This
theme is interpreted in two distinct but complimentary ways
in the Bible. There is that judgement which is built into the
order of things; '. . . whatever a man sows, that will he also
reap' (Gal. 6:7). But there is also the assertion of an end-time
of judgement. We read that God, '. . . will judge the world in
righteousness . . .' (Acts 17:31). And this judgement will be
according to Jesus Christ. These two strands of thought,
present and future judgement related to Christ, are sometimes
held together by speaking of eschatology, the doctrine of the
last things. By this we mean that the entry of Jesus Christ into
human history introduced a new state of affairs. His presence
in human life, at a particular point in time, marks the beginning of a new era. In Him God is uniquely revealed, through
His life, death and resurrection God's loving answer to the
problems created by man's sinfulness is demonstrated. In the
events of His life the Kingdom of God is inaugurated on
earth (see Mark 1:15; Matt. 12:28; Luke 11:20). Man now has
provided for him a norm by which to understand God, a way
by which to approach God, a pattern by which to live for God.
It is the decisive turn in human affairs. As John's Gospel has it,
'light has come into the world' (John 3:19). This light, in
Christ, introduced the decisive end-time in which we are now
living, in which men can apprehend, and be apprehended by
God's revelation of Himself and His salvation in Christ. To
live in this end-time is therefore a privilege and a responsibility.
We may live in the light and be saved in so doing but we may
also reject the light and be judged by it as we do so. The end-
time is a crisis time in which the crucial decision is that for or
against the light revealed in Christ. As Stephen Travis puts it,
'Ever since, whenever men have been confronted by Christ
and his gospel, they have responded to him or turned from him.

But men's response to Jesus *is* their response to God, and in making up their minds about him they bring judgment or salvation upon themselves. Nothing could be plainer than John's insistence that judgment is self-imposed.'[11] After examining biblical evidence for the ideas of present and future judgement (pp. 10–18), Travis concludes, 'Thus we can understand the link between judgment in the present life and judgment at the last day. The final judgment means God's underlining and ratification of the relationship towards him which we have chosen in this life. If we have fellowship with God now, we shall enter into a fuller experience of his presence then. If we do not know him now, we shall not know him then' (p. 18).

To say that our worship is eschatological means, in this sense, that all our worship is carried out within the decisive end-time, and part of that end-time is judgement. This affects the directional element of our worship at a number of points.

It means, for example, that all our worship should be characterized by a sense of urgency. End-times are crisis times; we have no grounds for carelessness. Every moment, act and word is important, and needs to be meaningful. The matters in which we deal at worship are urgent. It also means that we shall have a real sense of being under divine judgement but for the grace of God. The lives we lead and the society in which we live are not of themselves worthy to be offered. They are only capable of becoming so through God's grace in Christ. The element of judgement will be an important part of our reflection upon life in worship. And it will also introduce the element of pilgrimage into worship. We are, as our forefathers used to sing, 'Marching to Zion'. This is not a concept involving ideas of the present world not mattering; of cutting ourselves off from it. These are abuses of the pilgrim idea. The pilgrim sense of the people of God has to do with direction and movement. It is an assertion that growth and development in the Christian life are both possible and necessary; that we seek to be more like the people God wishes us to be as week by week we meet in worship. And in that worship we look at ourselves as those who are answerable and who expect to be in process of change.

[11] *Preaching the Judgment of God*, Methodist Division of Home Mission Occasional Paper, 1973, p. 12.

Our doctrine of God is the first foundation of our worship. It provides the proper dimensions of worship, it lends points of reference to make worship meaningful, and it indicates the directions of worship. One final comment remains. If we attempt to work out the principles outlined above we shall face inevitable tensions within our worship. One is the tension between transcendence and immanence. Another concerns our celebration of the world and our awareness of its sinfulness. Yet another is the necessity to spend time in worship, balanced by the equally urgent necessity to get out into the world in God's service. We are called to offer grace, and yet we ourselves are in constant need of it ourselves. And so one could go on. Life is made up of a properly balanced experience of tension, and worship is no exception. To remove healthy tension may be the first step towards death. Truly to worship, on the foundation of the character of God, is not to solve tensions but to enter into the life which they express.

Chapter Two

THROUGH JESUS CHRIST

'No one has ever seen God; the only Son, who is in the bosom of the Father, he has made him known' (John 1:18). John draws our attention to the step which we must now take. Much of the material in the last chapter would be equally relevant to Jewish as to Christian worship. Each aspect of the being of God which we there described was perceived, however dimly and partially, by the people of the Old Testament. Our next question must therefore be, 'What is it that differentiates Christian worship from Jewish or any other kind of worship?' The answer is that it is offered 'through Jesus Christ'.

We may put the question in another way by asking, 'If the Jews knew so much about God, why was the coming of Jesus necessary at all?' The beginning of an answer is found in John's Gospel, 'In the beginning was the Word, and the Word was with God, and the Word was God' (John 1:1), or, as the New English Bible puts it, 'The Word dwelt with God, and what God was, the Word was'. To this we add the staggering statement later in the same chapter, 'And the Word became flesh and dwelt among us, full of grace and truth; we have beheld his glory, glory as of the only Son from the Father' (John 1:14).

In Jesus Christ John sees the embodiment of the reality of God. In the words of the Christmas story He is, 'Emmanuel . . . God with us' (Matt. 1:23). Paul says that '. . . in him all the fullness of God was pleased to dwell' (Col. 1:19). The writer to the Hebrews says, 'He reflects the glory of God and bears the very stamp of his nature' (Heb. 1:3). This is the testimony of the early Christians being transmitted in writing to us. What as Jews they had rightly grasped about God, as Christians they saw confirmed in Jesus Christ. Where, as Jews, they had misunderstood, or partially seen, or wrongly applied what they knew, as Christians they found Jesus Christ offering the

corrective.[1] He took the Law, cleared away their faulty
additions and misunderstandings, and revealed the Lawgiver
behind it. He took their sacrificial system and gathered it all
up into His own death upon the Cross. He received their
moral standards, with their scrupulous attention to outward
detail, and applied their principles to inner holiness.[2] No
wonder they wished to record His having said, 'He who has
seen me has seen the Father' (John 14:9).

The implications of this for our worship can hardly be
exaggerated. It means, first of all, that every act of worship has
a *firm rootage in history*. Dom Gregory Dix wrote, 'Christianity
is the only religion which actually *depends entirely upon history*.'[3]
Professor Mascall puts it even more starkly, 'Christianity . . .
stands or falls by certain events which are alleged to have taken
place during a particular period of forty-eight hours in Palestine
nearly two thousand years ago.'[4] Or to quote Eduard
Schweitzer, 'To the first church Jesus Christ was not an idea
but a sum of events.'[5] This all means that our worship does not
depend solely upon ideas about God but upon convictions
about God which have been tested against historical evidence
based on Jesus Christ. We do not come to worship simply to
share helpful and challenging concepts: we come to respond to
history. Our basic aim is not to explore and apply moral and
religious philosophy to ourselves and life about us, so much as
to relate ourselves properly to what God has already done in
history through Jesus Christ. 'The primary declaration of
Christianity is not "This Do", but "This Happened".'[6]

This means that much of our worship will necessarily be

---

[1] This is one way of understanding the purpose of the Sermon on the Mount in
Matthew 5–7. See, for example, Martyn Lloyd-Jones, *Studies in the Sermon on the
Mount*, Vols. 1 and 2, Inter-Varsity Fellowship 1959. Concluding part of his
exposition, he writes, 'It is the Spirit not the letter that matters; it is the intent,
object and purpose that are important. The one thing we have to avoid above
everything else in our Christian lives is this fatal tendency to live the Christian life
apart from a direct, living and true relationship to God' (Vol. 1, p. 220).

[2] For the way in which Jesus applied Old Testament material to Himself see
R. T. Francis, *Jesus and the Old Testament*, Tyndale Press 1971.

[3] *Jew and Greek: A Study in the Primitive Church*, Dacre Press 1953, p. 5.

[4] E. L. Mascall, *Theology and History*, Faith Press 1962.

[5] *Lordship and Discipleship*, S.C.M. 1960, p. 96 (though note Schweitzer's following
point, that the events are 'historic', that those most emphasized are least capable of
historical examination and are statements of faith).

[6] Evelyn Underhill, *Worship*, p. 68.

taken up with acts of corporate memory; of recalling what is the basis of our faith in history. If our services—in the laudable search for modernity and relevance—omit sufficient recollection of our beginnings, they will be in danger of moving us from the only foundation we have, Jesus Christ Himself. Paul had hard things to say about building anywhere else (I Cor. 3:10–15). Congregations, and those who conduct their worship, must exercise great care that everything in our worship is Christian in this sense. Exciting new Christian ideas need to be tested against the evidence of God's definitive revelation in Christian.[7] 'Faith is not something which men have invented for their comfort; it is something which has been created by God's action in history, not our achievement but his gift. One certain and indisputable fact about Christian origins is this: that faith in God the Father was made possible, not for Israel only but for all mankind, by the historical fact of Jesus Christ.'[8] To use theological shorthand, the Christ of our faith must be seen to be the Jesus of our history. Loss of memory is every bit as serious for a worshipping community as for an individual in everyday life. In either case the result is usually a slide into fantasies which are further and further removed from reality.

Yet this in no sense commits the Church to fulfilling the role of antiquarian society, whiling away its days in recalling the past and its glories. God's revelation of Himself in history was an affirmation of history, a divine declaration that the historical is a fitting avenue along which the divine will may be revealed, divine purposes worked out. We rightly expect that all His activity would be consonant with His unique and definitive revelation of Himself in Jesus Christ; but we need not expect that all that He has to teach us has already been discovered,

[7] Interestingly one of the recent books on early Christian worship, Ferdinand Hahn, *The Worship of the Early Church* (Eng. trans. David E. Green: ed. John Reumann) argues that the key to the pattern of early Christian worship is the outlook of Jesus Himself. Hahn argues that Jesus exercised freedom as well as feeling constraint in relation to the Jewish tradition of worship. Specifically, Hahn argues, Jesus made a decisive break with the sacralizing, cultic framework of Jewish worship and placed it in the setting of everyday life. We need not concern ourselves at this point with the details of this thesis. What *is* relevant, however, is the point that it was Jesus' outlook which was normative, and which gave Christian worship its distinctive quality. Is there any reason—bearing in mind the relationship of Christianity to Christ—why it should not still be the case?

[8] Alan Richardson, *Four Anchors from the Stern*, S.C.M. 1963, p. 12.

fully understood and properly applied. The link between our historical rootage and our present acts of worship is our understanding of history as linear (it is going somewhere), and our belief about God (that He is consistent). This means that what He has done once in history through His Son still has relevance for us, and will require all our devotion and attention if we are to understand its general significance for all men and all ages, and its particular significance for us and our age. Our worship will not only reflect upon our historical basis, therefore; it will need to reflect also upon the significance of that divine act in Christ for today, for us and our world. To neglect either kind of reflection—historical or existential—in favour of the other, is to threaten the meaningfulness of our worship. God's activity in Christ is the paradigm of His work among men; it is the basic equation. Paradigms and equations, however, are for application in all the relevant areas to which they relate. Recalling and relating are vital points in the rhythm. To quote Evelyn Underhill once more, 'Thus Christian worship is focussed on the eternalization of an historical fact, accepted as the revealing medium of divine truth, and this means that each phase and aspect of this historical fact, this unique life—each state and act and word of Jesus . . . —carries spiritual significance, points beyond itself, and opens for the believer a door upon Eternity. Each is a disclosure of the Logos, and therefore an invitation to worship.'[9] This may properly lead us to ask whether our worship contains a proper balance between recalling the historical and reflecting the existential.

An illustration of the way in which the historical and the existential (corresponding to the acts of recalling and relating in our worship), operate in harmonious counterpoint with one another is afforded by a series of almost simultaneous experiences of the writer a number of years ago. I was on my way to preach at an open-air gathering—and was a little short of time—when I met a sign which said 'Slow down, narrow bridge, right-angle bend'. Each of the descriptions was perfectly accurate; had I not slowed down I would have gone straight through a gate marked 'keep this gate shut'! Now that kind of evidence is presumably still available, and one could therefore

[9] *Worship*, pp. 69–70.

take any doubter to the precise spot and show the notice, the bend, the bridge and the gate. Plainly the historical events at the base of the Christian life cannot afford this kind of 'proof'. We cannot simply 'go back' and see it all again for ourselves, and many who did witness the life of Jesus Christ did not believe, anyway.

Having negotiated the bend and the bridge I found myself on a narrow road travelling behind a Ford Anglia car which was in no hurry at all. Its age was evident both from its appearance and because in the back window it had a bill, in black and white stripes, with the caption 'The Magnificent Magpies'. North-easterners will know that the 'Magpies' are Newcastle United Football Club. At the time of the incident here described, Newcastle United were a competent side; they were in no sense magnificent. When the car was bought, however, they undoubtedly were! Their record shows this. The historical evidence from which Christianity springs is not to be viewed in this way, either. It is not something which once was true (United *were* magnificent!) and which, given time, might become true again (United are building up their team!). By definition, and by the nature of its claims—that God has revealed Himself uniquely and once-for-all in the person and work of Jesus Christ—the historical basis of Christianity needs to be *permanently* valid and true. But how can we know it to be the case?

When, finally, I passed the Ford Anglia, with its message of former glories and future hopes, I found myself behind a motorcoach. On the back was the name of a person (in the plural) and a place. In literal terms, therefore, one could have been excused for assuming that all the passengers bore that name and came from that place. As I passed the coach, however, there were other indications available. Most of the people travelling were wearing a dark uniform. The men had peaked caps, some with red bands around them and some blue. A variety of shaped cases could be seen. Some ladies were wearing bonnets. By the time I had passed the coach I was fairly sure that this was a Salvation Army band, and that it was travelling to the same place and would be playing at the service where I was to speak. I was *fairly* sure; but not certain. In the situation the only thing to do was to proceed to the spot indicated. Not

long after my arrival the coach turned up too, and my hypothesis was confirmed. What I had thought to be the case, on
the basis of evidence and its significance, was shown to be the
case in experience as one went to the place where it could be so
shown.

The historical evidence about Jesus Christ in the New
Testament helps us in a similar way. But in order to appreciate
this we need to be clear about three related, though separate,
elements in its relationship to us. The first is the description of
events. Jesus Christ was born; He taught; He was put to death,
and so on. But the second element is constantly entering in,
namely, the interpretation. Jesus Christ was born—an *event*—
but it *means* 'Emmanuel . . . God with us' (Matt 1:23), for He is
'the exact representation of (God's) being' (Heb. 1:3 New
International Version), 'the image of the invisible God',
because 'in him all the fulness of God was pleased to dwell'
(Col. 1:15, 19). He is the eternal word, become flesh to dwell
among us (John 1:14). In the same way He is described as
teaching and healing—historical events—but their meaning
relates to the inaugurating of the kingdom of God (Mark 1:15;
Matt 12:28; Luke 11:20). His death is recorded as an event,
but its significance has to do with the battle against evil in the
world (Acts 2:23; Col. 2:15), with a demonstration of God's
love (Rom. 5:8; II Cor. 5:14), sovereignty (Acts 2:23; Mark
14:36 and parallels) and righteousness (Rom. 3:21–26), and
with God's offer to man of forgiveness (Col. 2:13), reconciliation (II Cor. 5:18–21) and liberation (Rom. 6:1–14).

The inter-relation of event and interpretation is not a simple
one,[10] but we cannot dismiss either totally without making a
fundamental change in the nature of Christianity itself, and
particularly in its view of the way God relates to the world and
reveals Himself in history.

But there is a third element, namely, invitation. The events

[10] There is a large area of debate among scholars concerning the status as
historical record of some of the gospel material. Two points are in place here. The
first is that because the gospel writers did not write history as modern historians do,
but rather ordered their material to make certain theological points, the historicity
of that which they so ordered is not necessarily called into question. The second
point is that however scholars vary, all admit the presence of some historical
material alongside or as part of the interpretation. The major debate is about how
much is historical, how much interpretative, and how to distinguish one from the
other. This debate does not therefore invalidate the argument being pursued here.

described do not prove anything. The *descriptions* of the death of Jesus Christ, for example, are not of themselves proof that He was and is the unique Son of God. Certain details in the descriptions, if accepted as historical, are plainly meant to indicate something very special. Yet they are not proof. But the *interpretations* move us further forward, for in these we begin to understand why the event is described, why it is given such a comparatively large part of the space in the Gospels, and why there are unusual elements in the accounts themselves. The events are portrayed as containing within them divine activity, passing judgement on sin, defeating the evil forces operating in the world, demonstrating the endless and bottomless love of God, making available forgiveness and reconciliation.[11] The events described are thus signposts pointing us to the truth about God and about the realities of life. And here the *invitation* is made. Just as I had to go to the place where I would discover whether or not the travellers in the coach were Salvation Army bandsmen, so, alongside the 'happenedness' of the events, and the probability of their interpretations, there is required the individual willingness to take up the invitation; to explore personally how far the events and interpretations accord with life and its meaning, its problems, its potential. Are the evils which Jesus warned against, such as living to oneself (Luke 12:16–21), ignoring the needs of others (Luke 10:30–37), being dominated by the desire for material possessions (Matt. 6:25–33) or the praise of men (Matt. 6:2–18), living as though only that which responds to the senses is real (Matt. 6:19–21), manipulating other people for our own ends and treating them as less than persons (Matt. 23:13–39), concentrating on a man's outward performance rather than his inner state (Matt. 5:21–30); are these relevant to one's present condition and the condition of the world? Does what Jesus offers—the knowledge of God as Father (Matt. 6:25–33), peace (John 14:27), a power at work within one's personality through the life of the Spirit within (John 3:1–8), gaining life by offering it in service of Christ and the gospel (Mark 8:35)—do these things meet our need? And do the wider visions of Christianity excite our hopes and liberate our personalities? Are the qualities revealed in Christ the clue to living because they are planted at the heart

[11] See earlier references in this chapter.

of Creation? (Col. 1:16; Heb. 1:2; John 1:3). Are love, truth, trust, self-giving and a sense that nothing in this life is absolute except God, out of whose hands nothing else can take us (Rom. 8:28–29)—are these the very stuff of life? Then if I think it at least to be possible, how can I find out? The invitation includes the details, couched in many different forms in the New Testament itself, 'Repent and believe' (Mark 1:15), 'Repent and be baptized' (Acts 2:38), 'Call on the name of the Lord' (Acts 2:21), 'Come unto Me' (Matt. 11:28), 'Become a new creation in Christ' (II Cor. 5:17), 'Be born anew' (John 3:3, 7), 'Put off the old nature, put on the new' (Eph. 4:22–24), 'Deny yourself, take up your cross, and follow me' (Mark 8:34). All have one thing in common; they involve the commitment of oneself to God in Christ as a faith response of the whole person, against the canvas of the whole of life.

Event, interpretation and invitation call for examination, understanding and response. Here is one motif of our worship as it relates to historical foundations. We come in worship to be reminded about and to rejoice in the way in which God has involved Himself and acted in our history at a particular place and time and through a particular person. We come in worship to explore together and to celebrate the meaning of those historical events surrounding the Incarnation of Christ (one of which is that God is always active in time, places and persons, and that we recognize his activity by the norm of the unique revelation in Christ). And we come in worship to renew and deepen our response to the invitation contained in the events and their significance. In such a way the Jesus of history becomes for us the Christ of faith, and the Christ of faith is seen by us to be the Jesus of history—and our worship is both firmly rooted in past history and enriched in the present.

To affirm that worship is through Jesus Christ is also *to personalize worship*. Meaningful worship can, of course, derive help from many sources. Traditional forms, systems of thought, concepts, ideas and language all play their part. But beneath all these for the Christian, lies the truth of God revealed in a personal way through Christ. The harmonious dynamism of our worship is not expressed in the words, 'It coheres', but in the statement, 'He lives'. This is how it happened to the early disciples. They had their traditions, concepts, thought forms and words to describe their God. He was personal in the sense that He dealt with them, individually and corporately, in a personal way. Expressions of Fatherhood, Love, Faithfulness, Anger, all testified to their understanding of Him as personal, But when Jesus Christ entered into their lives a revolution took place.

Jesus did talk about God, and yet 'Teacher' seemed inadequate as a total description of what He was. He mended broken bodies in God's name, yet it would not do simply to call Him 'Healer'. They discovered, in fact, that none of their traditional categories would fit Him. In the end, the gospels tell us, they found satisfaction in accounting for Him only by equating Him with God in the language of verses like that with which we began this chapter (See also, e.g. Matt. 16:16; John 11:27). Jesus was, for the early Christians, the embodiment of all the attributes of God we were thinking about in the last chapter: transcendence, immanence, love, righteousness, holiness, creation, redemption and judgement are all present in their accounts of Him. At each of these points the link with the Old Testament understanding of God is unmistakable. Yet Jesus does not simply illustrate these qualities of God as the Jews knew Him: He revolutionizes and transforms them within His own person.[12] In Jesus Christ they saw, as they had never seen before, what these characteristics of God were really like; faithfulness which weeps, love which gives itself up to die, the creating word nailed by creatures to a part of the creation, transcendence and immanence fused indissolubly in one human life which is more than human. They almost end up by saying that 'God is like Jesus'.

William Barclay expresses it well with the words '. . . in Jesus we do not see the abstract God of the theologians and the philosophers; but we do see, perfectly and completely in full revelation, the Father, the attitude of God to men, *how God feels to me*. In Jesus there is fully displayed the mind of God to men.'[13]

In our attempt to assess the quality of our worship we shall be wise to explore the significance of Jesus as the personal revelation of the Father. It may be that the complaints about worship being boring, irrelevant and unintelligible are all

[12] For an expression of this, see R. T. Francis, *Jesus and the Old Testament.*
[13] *By What Authority?*, Darton, Longman & Todd 1974, p. 107.

capable of orthodox answers which satisfy the minds of those who give them. Many such criticisms of worship can be dealt with by pointing to deficiencies in the concept of worship and in the preparation for worship of those who make them. Yet both the criticisms and their responses may have missed a deeper level of dissatisfaction with some of our worship—that it does not enable us personally to meet the Father. Yet this is precisely what the presence of Jesus did provide, even for those who were judged by His presence. How was the Father revealed in a personal way? If we understand that more clearly we may be better placed to see how worship 'through Jesus Christ' reveals the Father personally.

First, in Jesus God made Himself equally accessible to all kinds of people. One characteristic of the gospels is the diversity of people with whom Jesus dealt, at times to the surprise of onlookers. Each was accepted as a person with an individuality and a human dignity of his or her own, even though in some cases they had done much to forfeit such rights. Each is dealt with sensitively, and for each the implications of the kingdom of God are indicated. Some were not able to respond positively. The self-determination of none was attacked. The right of personal choice was honoured—but the need to choose, the implications of crisis, were made very plain.

He was accessible to crowds as well as to individuals—whether they were mothers with children or men in large numbers. The plan by his disciples to lessen His accessibility was rebuked (Mark 10:13–16). And the crowds, too, were treated in a way which made the need for response clear, but did not force such response. Their status as responsible, self-determining beings, with right and capability to accept or reject, to relate positively or negatively and face the consequences, was enhanced by being in His presence.

Secondly, He met people with an understanding of their nature and their circumstances, and began from there. Whether discussing water at a well (John 4:7–15), theology by night (John 3:7–15) or morals in broad daylight (Matt. 5:21–48), He left people in no doubt that He knew them and that the starting point was where they stood, even if the end point was far removed from it. It was His ability authoritatively and yet winsomely to meet each person and situation with a relevant aspect of the Kingdom of God which was so intriguing and compelling. The Father's care extends even to the sparrows and the grass so why not to every person? The invitation to pilgrimage, from where they stood to where He could take them, was never far away. Their lives could be enhanced or impoverished by their response or rejection: either way it was difficult to be simply the same as before. For He spoke with authority.[14]

Thirdly, He spoke in terms of familiar objects, events, customs and people. Each of these had a meaning and significance of its own. Thus people could hear His stories, listen to His teaching and yet not become committed to Him. They interpreted it all at face value, as we say. Others perceived, however, that beneath the familiar language about sowers and builders, housewives and shepherds, fathers and bridesmaids, masters and servants there was a less familiar meaning, an inner significance relating to the Father and His ways with His children, the Creator and His ways with His creatures, the Kingdom of God and its relationship to the kingdoms of this world. Disturbed and perplexed by this glimpse of inwardness they returned to Jesus for interpretation, only to discover that often He Himself stood at the centre of so many of His sayings and parables.[15] On other occasions it is the Father who is obviously the clue to the story. In this way the story quickens the sense of personhood in the hearer by involving him in itself and by offering a relationship if response is forthcoming.

Fourthly, the nature of the response involved was made clear. Whether in terms of repentance and faith, or self-denial leading to freedom, it is described in a way which implies total commitment. This is brought out in the appeal of the stories Jesus told. They intrigue our minds, engage our wills, stir our emotions. It is made abundantly clear also by the lists of those aspects of the disciple's life which are to take second place to Jesus Christ Himself—father, mother, wife, children, brothers, sisters, possessions, one's own life (Luke 14:25–33). It seems clear that

[14] Barclay, op. cit., ch. 3 'The Authority of Jesus'.
[15] On the sayings of Jesus in general see A. M. Hunter, *The Work and Words of Jesus*, S.C.M. 1950. On the relationship of Jesus to the Parables one notes how frequently the 'I am' sayings of John's gospel use themes made familiar in the other gospels via the parables—Shepherd, Door, Bread, Vine—but apply them to Jesus Himself. (This link was suggested some years ago by Professor H. N. Reisenfield of Uppsala.)

such teaching was not meant to produce an 'inventory mentality' ('how much shall I hand over?'), but rather to show that such reckoning is itself irrelevant in the Kingdom, for here only the giving of persons is meaningful. This is surely the point of those accounts of Jesus dealing so firmly with those who wished to be disciples but had other duties to see to first (Luke 9:57–62). The Father's call, through the Son, was for now and for all.

If we attempt to relate all this to our worship we must begin by admitting (or protesting!) that it is all so much harder for us. To begin with, we are not Jesus and most of us would not claim to understand human nature as He did. Moreover our world has come a long way since the first century. Life is more complex, knowledge more extensive, choices more varied, cultures more fragmented, religious interpretations of life more suspect. So one could go on. Yet however much more difficult the task may be, this element of the personalizing of worship is probably more important today than ever, when the 'global village' concept leaves many human beings with great doubt about their personal identity or value.

We may begin with God's 'accessibility' through Jesus. Of course we can know, intellectually, that God is present in our worship (either because He is present everywhere, or because we believe it to be so on the basis of His nature or promises). But is it so wrong to wish for a *sense* of His presence too?[16] Those who met Jesus did not mostly—we may assume—begin with an intellectual concept of God's accessibility through the wandering teacher. Yet many of them *became aware* of the presence of God, and responded by professions of faith, pleas for forgiveness, promises of restitution or agonized cries (John 20:28; Luke 5:8, 19:8; Mark 5:7). It was more than an intellectual exercise: there was a challenge to emotion and will; there were decisions to be made, conditions to be put right, actions to be taken, responses to be offered. Persons, in their personhood, felt God to be confronting them in a way which made response necessary, possible and urgent.

How often would this be a true description of our worship today? We are back to the contrast between Barth's definition

---

[16] For a spirited defence of this position see Martin Thornton, *My God: A reappraisal of normal religious experience*, Hodder & Stoughton 1974, especially chapters 1–3.

of worship and our description of it, in the introduction. Is it possible to indicate any ways in which we have lost the personalizing influence of Jesus Christ upon our worship?

One suggestion could be worked out as follows. In the days when the gospels were largely viewed as biographies, talk about the Jesus of History could be confident. True it was admitted that we lacked a lot of information, particularly about His early life, but also about the time of His ministry, and about matters of physical appearance, for example. But the picture was clear, and could be portrayed by artists and dramatists, as well as by Sunday School teachers and preachers. People believed they knew to whom they were relating. Doubts about the historical (as opposed to historic) authenticity of many of the gospel accounts as descriptions of what actually happened or was said, which have been one part of the critical New Testament scholarship of the past century, have made serious in-roads into this belief and experience. If we cannot be sure that He did do and say certain things; if all we have is a construction (variously assembled) by the early Church, how can we be sure to *whom* we are relating? Under such pressure Jesus Christ seems more like an idea—or a collection of ideas—than a person.

The situation is further complicated by the influence of some critical scholarship upon Christian views of the resurrection of Christ. If the physical resurrection of Jesus Christ is denied, and the so-called 'mythological structure' laid on one side in the interests of discovering the 'abiding truth' contained in the stories; then we are again in the area, not of persons but of ideas. Resurrection is not now 'something which happened to Jesus Christ' (nor therefore, presumably, to anyone else—despite Paul and I Corinthians 15!); rather it is a mythological way of describing an abiding truth about things as they are with God, a truth outstandingly revealed in Jesus.

It is perhaps not surprising that the past few years have produced a variety of 'new' attempts to relate to Jesus. A 'death of God' theologian sees Him as 'a place to be'.[17] A New

---

[17] 'For the radical Christian, Hamilton suggests, Jesus is not so much the object or ground of faith as he is a "place to be", a standpoint' (Thos. W. Ogletree, *The 'Death of God' Controversy*, S.C.M. 1966). For the details see Thomas J. J. Altizer and William Hamilton, *Radical Theology and the Death of God*, Pelican 1968, pp. 36–62 'The Death of God Theologies Today'.

Testament scholar argues that we must work on the basis of the 'character or spirit of Christ'.[18] In the field of Christology emphasis is now moving to the humanity of Christ as the clue to His person.[19] By contrast, one might almost say as a viable alternative, the 'Jesus People' are seeking to re-create the first century life-style of Jesus and His followers in a twentieth-century setting.[20] The Charismatic Movement proclaims that the baptism of the Holy Spirit makes Jesus real, so that they too are 'a Jesus Movement'.[21]

This is not the place to embark upon lengthy examinations of canons of biblical interpretation and methods of theological enquiry; but it is relevant at this point to ask whether worship *can* be truly Christian which does not lay stress upon Jesus Christ as a person to whom Christians today can offer their allegiance, and through that allegiance know and serve God. May it not be that much of our worship lacks life because worshippers do not sense the presence of God; and that they do not become so aware because we neglect the person of Jesus Christ as the one through whom the Father became and becomes personally accessible?

We may take the next two points together—His ability to begin where He knew people to be, and the way in which He used familiar words, stories, situations and experiences as pointers to the Kingdom of God. Here it is easy to be misled into an apparently simple solution—abolish all technical religious language, talk and pray only about essentially every-day matters, confine oneself to what man is naturally capable of, and people will both feel at home in worship and respond to it. There may be other grounds on which to base such an argument, but the teaching and ministry of Jesus do not provide them. To begin with He *was* in fact able to use religious language. After all His hearers were extremely familiar with it. But what He did was to select what was relevant to His

---

[18] S. W. Sykes *Christian Theology Today*, Mowbray 1971.

[19] See, for example, David Welbourn, *God-Dimensional Man*, Epworth 1972.

[20] Roger C. Palms, *The Jesus Kids*, S.C.M. 1972.

[21] 'The Baptism in the Holy Spirit is the name given to a gift of God in the Holy Spirit in which a believer is made conscious of the indwelling presence of Christ and is empowered to make an effective witness to Christ in word and deed' (John Horner, quoted in William R. Davies and Ross Peart, *The Charismatic Movement and Methodism*—a Home Mission Occasional Paper 1973, p. 9).

message and ministry and fill it out significantly in His own way. Words like Son of Man, Kingdom of God, baptism, are possible examples. Thus even the religious language He used pointed people on beyond the previous understanding they had reached. (We may recall how well His followers learned the lesson, as their use of the Greek word *agape*—love—reveals.) His use of familiar religious words and thought forms enabled Him to show that the current conceptions of His hearers were either extremely limited or in other cases in error. His use of their wrong interpretations of the Law in Matthew's account of the Sermon on the Mount serves to illustrate this. Are we in danger, one wonders, of losing this insight by our passion for prosaic, immediately intelligible words on the one hand, and our concern for secular thought forms on the other? This way we forget the need to be pointed beyond the familiar to the unfamiliar and as a result we become locked up in secular frames of reference dictated by the world around us. Mystery, awe, encounter with an unseen world of hidden reality are all discounted in the interests of what can be openly demonstrated or explained in ordinary everyday terms. Claims of uniqueness are prohibited by the very criteria which are applied. Since any description of an event must be tested by parallel accounts of similar events, the unique event is precluded. Religious language as a signpost to hidden reality is soon discounted in such circumstances, as is religious interpretation of current secular events. It is not surprising if liveliness in worship is lost as a result.

Of course such comments raise very important questions, but at the heart of this discussion is the very basic question, 'Does the Risen Christ become a reality to us in our worship?' Even if some would disagree with the form of the argument above they will surely wish to face the implications of this question. It is said of the late Archbishop of York, Dr Cyril Garbutt, that he was on one occasion preaching in a small village church and a local reporter secured an interview just before the service. 'Well, Your Grace', he said, 'what are you going to talk to them about today?' (knowing the Archbishop's expertise concerning social questions). The Archbishop replied, 'I think I shall tell them about Jesus.'

In the third place, 'through Jesus Christ' provides *a pattern* for our worship. This is not in any sense to suggest that hidden beneath the New Testament evidence is a blueprint liturgy! Our worship is not made as easy as that for us (nor as predictable, for which we may be grateful!). But it is to suggest that the New Testament teaching about Jesus implies a certain rhythm which derives from the pattern of Christ's total ministry. Since Christ is the pioneer of our faith, and our pattern and example of obedient service which is well-pleasing to God, it should prove instructive for our worship to observe the rhythm of His ministry. It is understood in a variety of ways within the New Testament. An examination of two of them may encourage readers to seek for more.

We begin with the ancient Christian hymn, as it seems to be, which Paul includes in his letter to the Church at Philippi (Phil. 2:6–11). We have here what one might call the parabola of God's action in Christ. From equality with God, Jesus Christ is portrayed as humbling Himself in Incarnation and Death: but God raises Him up and establishes His pre-eminence, that all may confess His Lordship. We have the same majestic sweep—from God to man and back again via Cross and Resurrection and Exaltation—as in John's gospel is portrayed by 'glorification'. At a number of points in that gospel Jesus is recorded as having spoken about glorification. It seems to include the total range of His ministry and all that followed it, as one great redemptive event. Here again the motif of the Philippians passage is worked out; but this time in terms of actual points in the ministry and teaching of Jesus. Spatial concepts can help us here, even if we are no longer tied to any literal understanding of them in Christian theology (if anyone ever was; which we may be pardoned for doubting!). From divine glory to earthly humiliation in the service of the Father and then back again via the obedience of the Cross and the vindication by God which followed is a brief description of the pattern involved. How little our worship relates to that kind of movement today! We are so (rightly) concerned about relevance and experience-centredness that our acts of worship seem to begin, continue and end in a miasma of anthropological reflections. At worst we mourn our failures; at best we consider the needs of other men. This has been for some an avenue along which they have found Christ, but only because they first knew *of* Him from some other source. Certainly it cannot function as the major path to Christ. But throughout it is human life and existence; human thought and its potential; human endeavour and its possibilities, which engage our attention. The experience of life we bring with us to worship not only provides the starting point for our worship, it often prescribes the limits also. Like a discussion group in which no one wishes to learn from anyone else, but all are determined to 'have their say', we go round and round our problems from a variety of angles, remaking our promises to ourselves and our fellows to do better, and then leaving with renewed determination but very little inspiration. To use the language of piety, 'heaven has not broken in'. To put it bluntly, 'God remains in the gallery'.

This approach is wrong for a whole set of reasons. In the first place it ignores the fact that divine grace precedes human perception and response. God is gracious whether or not I grasp that truth and am open to it, though of course the fact that *someone* has experienced His graciousness makes it a more meaningful concept. Christ lived, died and rose again for me whether or not I know it to be true and respond accordingly. There is an objectivity of grace quite apart from our subjective experience of it. Our worship needs therefore to begin by a reaching out for an understanding of the nature of God—a celebration of the deity, an awareness of God's presence, a reflection upon what that means. This is precisely how the Lord's Prayer begins—'Our Father who art in heaven'; a simple yet breathtaking description of two major attributes of God—love and majesty.

But to be so taken up with ourselves in worship is wrong for another reason. It neglects the fact that a sense of God, an appreciation of the holy, an awareness of the numinous, is also part of human experience. Relevant worship does not have to begin, continue and end with concentration upon politics, work, family and practical service. Neither ought it to be entirely taken up with spiritual soundings, search for an experience, endless request prayers. It should begin with, and be characterized by an awareness of God, a present experience of the meaning of His activity in history and the character thus revealed. This is a genuine human experience in the twentieth century as in any other. It should therefore be prepared for, expected and enjoyed by faith. There is no better beginning for worship.

We then follow the downward sweep of the parabola in humiliation as we both bemoan and celebrate humanity in its present state. Our worship here should be neither too optimistic nor too pessimistic. The Incarnation of the Word both affirms and judges our humanity, with its potential and its fallenness. As with the baptism of Jesus, so in our worship there is an identification of ourselves with the world as it is today—its slums, its discrimination, its hunger, despair and fragmentation: and also with its power, excitement and potential. There may need to be a point in our worship where we reach rock bottom, where we echo the cry of despair from the Cross, expressing the apparent forsakenness of God's people in the midst of so much that gives pain and disappointment. As for our Lord in Gethsemane, so for His followers now, there can be no running away from such a path.

But the parabola must begin its upward sweep some time! Certainly we identify ourselves with a lost and sinful world, for we belong to it. Undoubtedly we feel the agony of the Cross of Christ, for we seek to enter into it. But by faith we see another side to the Cross—its culmination of Christ's battle with the powers of evil; its declaration of the extent of God's love for sinners; its provision of the way of forgiveness, restoration, cleansing and renewal. It stands not only for the depths to which human life can sink in crucifying God's Son, it also stands for God's redeeming love, an event quite apart from me in time which nevertheless gathers me by faith into itself, till I can say with Paul, 'I am crucified with Christ'. At the lowest point of the parabola there is already a glimmer of hope.

Our worship may now move on from the Cross and its meaning to the Resurrection and its significance. Our worst enemies cannot hold us; that which we fear most—evil, failure, disease, death—cannot shut us in. Christ is Risen! Our worship moves into the great upward sweep as we celebrate the triumph of the Risen Christ—victorious over the forces of evil, successful in opening the way for those who will follow it into God's presence, free from the limitations of space and time; now to be with His people everywhere and anywhere; gloriously present

—now! The swell of joy, praise, deliverance and thankfulness should be explosive in our worship, for He is Risen!

And ascended. God's approval is given; His plan is fulfilled. We know that Christ's work was not a random effort by a zealous young Jew, nor the final fling of a revolutionary; it was the obedient act of the divine Son. His ascension assures us that He is accepted—and so are we, in Him. Therefore with gladness and with confidence we offer ourselves afresh as part of the redeemed community, the people of the Lord, moving both in and on to eternity with Him. We expect heaven to begin now, and as we face the life of the world we do not leave that atmosphere behind. As the chorus affirms, 'Where Jesus is, 'tis heaven there.'

Of course to leave the worshipper 'in the heavenlies' is out of keeping with much teaching about worship today. It is feared that to do so is to cause a false piety, a carelessness about the world and its problems, an impracticality of Christian life, and grave disappointment when high hopes are not fulfilled. In fact the opposite is true. When worship ends on the high note of the ascension our earthly problems are put into their right perspective. We are now better prepared to face them than we were when we came to worship, for we perceive their true proportion now. Moreover, to catch a glimpse of the triumph of Christ is to wish for all the world to enjoy the benefits and also to feel equipped to join in the task of making it so. Too often our worship is so concerned with our problems, resources and duties that we miss the vision of Christ's victory and send ourselves away more burdened than ever. Yet His triumph is the only clue to our situation—we cannot do His will any other way than by catching the vision and sharing His victory. Too often we leave worship with shoulders bent; when we ought to be walking with heads high, because of what He has done.

The other great value of ending worship on this note is that it sends us out with hope for the future. Christ's ascension and His return are closely connected. The 'Christ pattern' of worship sends us out in responsibility and hope. Responsibility because we are called to be ready for His coming, and to seek to have everyone else ready; hope because we know that the consummation of all God's promises lies out in the future, for 'hope' in the biblical sense means the confident expectation of something promised but not yet fulfilled. The sense of moving out of worship as part of our total movement towards the final point is the way to become involved in daily life again.

In the fourth place 'through Jesus Christ' *provides our worship with firm anchorage*. We can see this worked out in terms of Covenant. In the Old Testament we read of the covenant theme in the successive calls of Abraham (Gen. 12, 15, 17 and 22); we find the covenant theme again as one of the main bulwarks of Jewish history. Sometimes the prophets use it as the basis for criticism of the unfaithfulness of the Jews: at other times it is the ground for the prophet's assurance that God will never forsake His people, the people of the covenant.

When Jesus wished to communicate to His disciples the meaning of His coming death, it was to this theme that He turned. During the Last Supper, in which His death was prefigured, He is recorded as saying, 'This is my blood of the (new) Covenant' (Mark 14:24). For people who knew the intimate connection between sacrifice and Covenant, there could hardly have been a more striking indication of what Christ intended. The permanent divine assurance that forgiveness is now totally available was to be provided by the death of the divine Son Himself.

At the base of 'through Jesus Christ' worship therefore there is a glad certainty. We do not worship a fickle deity—'first he loves me then he doesn't'. Nor is the atmosphere meant to be one of 'on–off' Christianity—'sometimes I am and sometimes I'm not'. Nor is it a matter of my emotions—'He isn't with me because I can't always feel Him'. Worship cannot flourish permanently in any of these atmospheres. Rather we come to a covenant God; one who has declared His faithfulness and has sealed the declaration in the death of His own Son as the sign of how far His faithful love will go. The promise and the people of the promise are established by the blood of the Covenant. No wonder the hymn-writer wrote:

> 'Now I have found the ground wherein
>   Sure my soul's anchor may remain—
> The wounds of Jesus, for my sin
>   Before the world's foundations slain;

Whose mercy shall unshaken stay,
When heaven and earth are fled away'.

M.H.B. 375 v. 1

The being of God brings to our worship its dimensions, its reference points and its direction. In Jesus Christ we find these historically based and personalized. We also discover patterns of worship and a firm covenant security. But how does all this come to life week by week? We take that step in our next chapter.

Chapter Three

BY THE HOLY SPIRIT

'NEVERTHELESS I tell you the truth: it is to your advantage that I go away, for if I do not go away, the Counsellor will not come to you; but if I go, I will send him to you. And when he comes . . .' (John 16:17–18). We come now to one of the most crucial questions about worship, namely, what can we reasonably expect to happen? The problems preventing an easy answer are many. We live nearly two thousand years after Jesus Christ, so there is a time barrier. Palestine is far from Britain anyway, so there is a space barrier. Our society is very different from that which Jesus knew, so there is a cultural barrier. Our thought-forms and vocabulary bear little resemblance to those of the time of Jesus, so there is a communications barrier. And so one could go on. How can we—in face of such problems—expect much from twentieth-century worship? Perhaps no single question has threatened to sever the nerve of our Christian worship more than this one.

It is here that our opening quotation from John's gospel can help us. The writer of the gospel, recording his story later than the other gospel writers, and reflecting upon the presentation of the truth about Jesus in a different setting from that in which the events took place, is already beginning to face some of the problems with which we now have to come to terms. The sayings and deeds of Jesus here recorded are therefore particularly relevant, and none more than the words of Jesus about 'going away' and sending 'the Counsellor'.

In essence the problem for the disciples highlights ours today. While Jesus was physically present with them most of their difficulties were met. They could relate to Him as to one another, for He was there to be spoken to, touched and seen. The words He used sounded thoroughly familiar, the illustrations recognizable and relevant. If there were things they did not understand they could at least ask Him. If the application of His teaching was not immediately evident the Master was there to make it. Everything seemed to hang upon His physical presence with them. Then the bombshell dropped—He was going away; the tragic events to which He had referred from time to time were now to come to pass. He was to leave them. Their sense of gloom showed both in their silence and in their faces. But they had an even greater shock to come. He now asked them to understand that it was actually *better* for them if He went away. Only so could the Counsellor—the Holy Spirit —come. And when He comes . . . chapters 14 to 16 of John's gospel list some of the activity which they could expect once the Spirit had truly come. Expectancy was to be the keynote of their attitude for the future. From the Day of Pentecost onward we see in Acts the expectancy not only increased but also satisfied.

Now we must ask how this could be and of what use it is to us anyway. And the answer begins with the obvious assertion that the Christian faith will no longer be accessible only to those who can know the physical presence of Christ. He is to be capable of being known, through the work of the Holy Spirit, in varying times, places and cultures. Yet, secondly, the Jesus Christ who will so be known in such different circumstances will be the One whom His disciples knew. The Spirit, Jesus said, will testify to Christ, will remind them of His words, will guide them into the truth. To use theological jargon, the Jesus of History and the Christ of Faith are one and the same person. So we have a constant point of reference in our knowing of Jesus today. We can test our experiences and our expectations by the evidence of the New Testament. We are not left to cross an uncharted sea of diverse and unrelated religious experiences without map or compass. And all this is 'better' for two reasons. In the first place it makes Christ accessible in any place at any time, and in all places at all times. In the second place it means that to come to know Jesus at all is already to be introduced to a whole new area of unseen reality. It is also in John's gospel that we have the record of Jesus telling the (now believing) Thomas, 'Blessed are those who have not seen and yet believe' (John 20:29). This does not mean 'have believed without evidence', as is sometimes suggested today, but 'have entered a new sphere of life where, by faith, unseen realities are perceived and the Risen Christ is known'. Paul makes a similar point in II

Corinthians 5:17 where he is describing both his inner motivation for evangelism and also his message; both of which can
only be received by faith union with Christ. 'Therefore, if
anyone is in Christ, he is a new creation; the old has passed
away, behold, the new has come.' The Holy Spirit is the link
between the Jesus of History and the Christ of Faith; He is also
our link between the seen realities of our everyday existence
and the unseen realities of the life of faith; of life in Christ with
the new dimension it brings. In other words, if we are to understand the meaning and implications of the Christian faith only
the Holy Spirit can teach us, and without response to His work
we shall never understand it. This is why understanding and
faith are so closely linked together in New Testament thought,
as in Hebrews 11:3, for example: 'By faith we understand. . . .'
Expectancy in worship is not only possible, therefore, in any
time or place, it is a vital part of our faith, a process of co-
operation with the Holy Spirit whose task it is to teach us and
enrich us.

But what are we to expect? What is there to be expectant
about? Or is it to be just a vague expectancy of a meaningful
act, an edifying experience, or even a 'good time'? The answer
is that while each of these will properly play its part in the
effects of worship, we also have some very clear indications in
the New Testament of the specific work which the Holy Spirit
does. To these we must now turn.

The first may not be too welcome to us. The Holy Spirit
convicts of sin. Jesus promised that the Counsellor would so
apply the truths about Him (Jesus) that 'the world' would be
openly convicted. John (16:8–11) spells out the details. Sin,
righteousness and judgement are listed. The Spirit will take the
implications of the whole revelation in Christ and show people
what sin means; show by contrast what righteousness means;
and reveal the inevitability of judgement. In other words He
will make clear the realities of right and wrong in the sight of
God, will offer an alternative way, and will demonstrate the
dire consequences of taking the side of evil. Now this is not a
matter of whether or not preachers 'dangle people over the
jaws of Hell'. It has to do with basic assumptions which lie at
the heart of our faith. The awfulness of sin in God's world; the
clear contrast in God's righteousness revealed in Christ; and the

certainty of answerability for the way we choose: these do not depend upon the whim of the preacher; they are basic to our understanding anything else about the faith. And this the Holy Spirit is sent to teach us.

Having declared that these matters are not simply 'options' for those who conduct our worship, we must now go on to say that leaders of worship, and preachers, who are aware of the importance of this work of the Holy Spirit will wish to ensure that the act of worship provides for such elements to be included. Cranmer has been accused of being too much taken up with the presence of sin, but our worship will lose much reality without it. It is a matter of gratitude that most modern liturgies do find proper place for awareness, confession and assurance of forgiveness of sin. More will follow on the matter of righteousness. The element of judgement is greatly neglected today, though recent literature is leading back to a realization of its importance.[1] We may sum up this section by simply asserting that the task of the Holy Spirit is to disturb us in our worship; to turn our minds to the reality of evil and of our involvement in it, and to point us to a better way, to choices which lead us in the opposite direction.

Few will wish to ignore the over-emphasis upon sin which has given some preachers in some ages an unhealthy power over their congregations. Nor in our day, when we know steadily more about the nature and function of the human personality, should we wish to neglect the possibility of doing harm by attempts at creating guilt-feelings in our congregations. In some respects, however, our general unwillingness to refer to, explore the extent and meaning of, and seek forgiveness for sin may well be hindering the growth to wholeness of Christians today.

If we ignore the biblical emphasis upon sin as first and foremost an offence against God, for example, then we very quickly fall into the world's ways of relativizing sins, establishing lists of large, medium and small sins, and seeing them merely as matters of adjustment between human beings who are all involved anyway. We have only to contrast this view with that of Isaiah (Isa. 6:1–8) with his overwhelming sense of the majestic holiness of God, to see how far removed our culture is

[1] See, e.g. Stephen Travis, *Preaching the Judgment of God*

3

from seeing sin in its God-dimension. Yet if there is, at the heart of human life, a possibility of relationship between man and God, and if God is—as the Bible would lead us to believe— a holy God against whose nature sin is an offence, then plainly our worship must take this very seriously into account, or we shall be neglecting a problem at the heart of the relationship we are seeking to foster and express in worship.

Another failure at this level is our modern tendency to think of sins rather than sin; of acts, words, thoughts rather than of a condition which produces them. We are particularly conscious of social sins, of offences against our fellow-men, especially at the corporate level. If, however, we ignore the cause of these in our own individual personalities, and seek to put the situation right by fresh resolves to do more and better, we may well be like doctors treating symptoms rather than causes. One recognizes the need to be specific rather than to generalize about sin; but we must at the same time avoid that superficiality which views racism purely as a wrong view which can with education be corrected, rather than as one expression of the constant tendency of mankind (and therefore of men and women) to pride themselves over others, in the areas which S. D. Gordon described as pride of grace, race, face or place.[2]

We need also to recall that the biblical writers lay stress on man's responsibility for his sin. Sin is disobedience, and man— both corporately and individually—is accountable for it. One hastens to add that God's grace 'abounds all the more' as Paul puts it (Rom. 5:20). But quite apart from this there is a therapeutic element in helping man to accept his responsibility for that which is wrong. Simply to provide a number of heredi- tary and environmental reasons for acts of wrongdoing may well produce either carelessness or despair. There is a health-giving quality about the way in which the biblical teaching expects man to accept responsibility for sin—a necessary first step in the direction of discovering that God offers forgiveness and liberation in Jesus Christ; which leads us on to the second part of the Spirit's work.

We may also expect that the Holy Spirit will make Jesus real to us in our worship. Thus Jesus is recorded as asserting that, 'He will glorify me, for he will take what is mine and

[2] S. D. Gordon, *A Miscellany of Quiet Talks.*

declare it to you' (John 16:14). The task of the Holy Spirit thus includes helping us to see the significance of Christ. This is what Paul also declares, in a slightly different way (I Cor. 2:1–5). He says that he avoided clever talk or impressive words. He simply told them about the crucified Jesus Christ. Their faith, therefore, came about not because of human pressure, but because of the power of God by the Spirit. Are those of us who lead worship and preach, and those who attend worship, sufficiently expectant about the presence of the Holy Spirit to make Jesus a reality in our experience, to communicate to us the meaning of the gospel?

We have already considered some parts of the answer to this question, in the previous chapter. Here we may look at another part by asking whether we think on a large enough scale when we consider the significance of Jesus Christ. Our worship rightly helps us to focus upon the birth, life, death and resurrection of Jesus as key points in the gospel story. But the New Testament writers are not satisfied simply to recount these events and to offer interpretations of them. They go on to make assertions about Jesus Christ which require a faith response far greater than any of the miracle stories of the gospel.

Take, for example, the relationship established by John's gospel (1:1–3, 14), Paul in Colossians (1:15–17), and the writer of the letter to the Hebrews,[3] between Jesus Christ and the work of Creation. Quite apart from the difficulty modern scientific thought has with the concept of 'pre-existence', we have to come to grips with the claim that what was revealed in the earthly ministry of Christ is also at the heart of God's purposes in Creation. To take the next step from this is to assert that human life will only be fully experienced when those qualities supremely revealed in Jesus—love, obedience to the Father's will, concern for others, victory over evil, the establishing of righteousness on earth, and so on—are at the centre of man's relationships. This, in turn, gives pointers towards a proper response to the question of meaning which is both prevalent and perplexing in our modern world. But we shall not be able to address ourselves to such questions unless we have given proper consideration of, and explored together the implications of the christological basis of our answer. If our

---

[3] Hebrews 1:2 'through whom also he created the world' (lit. 'the ages').

worship is to be *meaning*ful we should surely spend some of it in just such consideration and exploration. By narrowing our christological basis we both impoverish our worship and limit our appreciation of life's meaning. In this way our worship is less related to modern questions than it might be. And we hinder the work of the Holy Spirit whose task it is to illuminate our understanding of Christ.

The same is true of the biblical teaching about the end-time, and the centrality of Jesus Christ in the New Testament concerning this matter. Again questions are raised by critical scholarship about the exact nature of New Testament teaching about eschatology and the end of the world. What is not in doubt, however, is the conviction of the earliest Christians that whenever or in whatever way history is to be wound up, the earthly ministry and significance of Jesus Christ is the supreme criterion for assessing its purpose and value. Here again there is a relationship to our modern world in which questions about the relative chances of the survival of our planet and of mankind upon it are being constantly raised. Allied to this is the question of how men ought to behave in such a setting and what purposeful goals should have priority in this situation. The Christian community has a challenge to witness by its contribution on these major issues, but we are not likely to do so unless our corporate experience as Christians—principally expressed in worship—enables us to do so. And it will not enable us, nor be related to this major area of modern perplexity, unless the christological key to questions of purpose and destiny is properly examined and employed.[4]

Yet again there is the way in which the New Testament writers view the Person of Jesus. The (at times) breathtaking contrasts between utter humanity and divine presence[5] pose a problem for every biblical scholar or theologian who wishes to assess all the evidence and reach logical conclusions which square with every piece of material available. There is little doubt, however, that the early Christians recognized in Jesus

[4] How is our attitude to and comment upon the future affected by such passages as Colossians 1:16 ('all things were made . . . for him'), Hebrews 1:2 ('heir of all things'), or Philippians 2:10 ('that at the name of Jesus every tree should bow')? For an interesting explanation in relation 'hope', see J. Moltmann, *A Theology of Hope*, S.C.M., 1967.

[5] See, e.g. Hebrews 1:1–4, and cf. Hebrews 2:10–18, 5:7–10.

a quality of human experience which they had never met before, and which they believed to be unique—of such a quality and so unique that only the ascription of divine Sonship really did justice to it.[6] Once more we are moving in an area of intense interest to modern man, whose knowledge of human behaviour and influences upon it poses the question of 'being' in an intense form. Equally, once more, the Church has a vital contribution to make, but will only make it in so far as it has itself adequately explored the christological content of its contribution, and entered into the implications for modern thought and action. Worship is one obvious point at which our being is perceived and expressed in relation to the being of God and in the setting of life in the modern world. And here the Spirit's help is promised.

One does not wish in the foregoing paragraphs to suggest that Christians have a simple solution to major modern problems; nor that the quotation of a few relevant biblical texts will somehow provide the answers and render unnecessary the agonizing thought, careful reflection and intense discussion which characterizes the search for truth in these matters. But it is to suggest that the Christian has, in Jesus Christ, the basic materials on which such understanding and solutions may be based.[7] But unless in our worship we are aware of this as the solution to our meaning, destiny and humanity it is difficult to see how we can proceed. And it ought to be present, not in order to 'enable us to witness', but because it lies at the heart of the basic questions we ourselves must ask. The central consideration is not, 'What will be its effect?' but 'Is it the pathway to truth?'. If, as the early Christians evidently believed, and successive Christian traditions have sought to confirm, it *is* such a pathway, then it ought to be present in our worship. And to miss or neglect it will be precisely to miss or neglect an important part of the Holy Spirit's witness to the significance of Jesus Christ.

A third part of our expectancy about the Holy Spirit's work concerns ourselves. What is He seeking to do for and in us? The

[6] See Matthew 16:13–20; Mark 8:27–30 and Luke 9:18–21 for the Synoptic Gospel writers' attempt to portray this awareness.

[7] For a further exploration of this point see Lesslie Newbigin, *The Finality of Christ*, S.C.M. 1969, especially ch. IV 'The Clue to History'.

list is a fairly extensive one, and as such it reminds us how
varied, rewarding and exciting our worship ought to be. We
may begin with His work for the deepening of faith. He is said
to be the source of the Christian's understanding (I Cor.
2:6–13). Here Paul argues that a man cannot, of himself,
understand the depths of God. (In passing one may wonder
whether the failure to accept this today, in the interests of
intellectual integrity or a limited view of what constitutes
knowledge, is not the greatest single hindrance to our growth
in mature understanding of God and of the faith.) Only the
Spirit, Paul argues, can understand the depths of God, and He
will declare them. Does our worship have about it the sense of
dependence upon the Spirit to reveal something more of God's
nature and ways to us? This in no sense means the sacrifice of
intellect; nor does it excuse hymn-writers, preachers and
listeners from the hard work of careful thought and responsible
expression. But it does remind us that our worship cannot
simply be described in terms of the sum of our thoughts, words
and activities. Full Christian worship is only possible on the
assumption that God the Holy Spirit is at work there to 'make
the depths of Godhead known'. Too often our worship becomes
a tiring exercise in self-help, because we have not learned the
art of receiving what He has to teach us.

In similar vein the Holy Spirit is said to lead us (Rom. 8:14).
The context is the battle within us between the 'flesh'—meaning
man in his susceptibility to sin, man vulnerable to temptation—
and the Spirit; not our spirit, but God's Holy Spirit who is at
work in our lives. He it is who gives us spiritual life (v. 10–11),
for He both raised Jesus from the dead and now dwells in the
believer. And He it is who will lead us as we seek to be done
with the powers of evil which seek to cause us to misuse and
abuse bodily desires. To be so led is to be seen to be a son of
God. How much of our worship takes this daily, personal and
sometimes fierce battle seriously? How much are we helped in
this daily warfare by the worship we attend? We should expect
that worship would afford new insights into the leading of the
Holy Spirit in this matter; new understanding of how we may
be more successful in the daily search for a truly Christian
quality of life. This is in no sense a demand for a return to a
narrow, inward-looking pietism. It is simply a recognition that

too often we neglect the area where above all the Christian battle is being fought—in the lives of the believers. If Christians are losing there they will have little effectiveness anywhere else. Large visions and great victories are built upon, not through the neglect of, faithful Christian living.

The Spirit is also said to give the Christian assurance in the faith. Paul goes on, in the same chapter of Romans, to affirm, 'When we cry "Abba! Father!" it is the Spirit himself bearing witness with our spirit that we are children of God . . .' (Rom. 8:15-16). This teaching has been greatly misunderstood. Some see it as sheer arrogance, since we have no right to be so sure of our salvation. Others see it as making in-roads into faith, since once you are assured of something you need no longer have faith about it. It has passed beyond the area where faith is necessary. But each of these is a misunderstanding. Assurance is a gift given *within the operation of faith*. It involves both taking God at His word, claiming His promises of salvation seriously, and experiencing on the ground of His promises the inner sense of being His child. If God has promised salvation in Christ to those who believe; and if I believe, then it is presumption *not* to expect assurance, since God can be trusted. It is not arrogance, for it depends wholly upon what God has done for us in Christ. Yet neither does it in any way dispense with faith, for it is a gift which is both received by faith, and which has as its content that which assumes the continuing presence of faith.[8]

Now we may ask again how much of our worship reflects this biblical insight into the Christian's experience? How often does our worship become the vehicle of a deeper (or a first awareness of) assurance that we are God's children through Jesus Christ? Christian growth, witness and service are all hindered without such an assurance, and we are robbed of much of our joy, for uncertainty attacks the roots of the Christian tree. Does our worship help those who sincerely lack assurance, and guide those who have it? When for example, did you last hear a sermon on assurance; or even sing a hymn which referred to it?

[8] See John Wesley 'The Witness of the Spirit', Sermon in *The Standard Sermons of John Wesley, Vol. I*, Annotated by E. H. Sugden, Epworth 1955. Also, from a different century and standpoint, see J. C. Ryle, *Holiness*, Jas. Clarke & Co. reprint 1956, Ch. VII, 'Assurance'. For an assessment of teaching on the subject, see A. S. Yates, *The Doctrine of Assurance*, Epworth Press 1952; and for a questioning of the doctrine as relevant today see John J. Vincent, *Christ and Methodism*, Epworth 1965.

Again, the Holy Spirit is said to help us in our prayers. Still in Romans 8, this time at verse 26, Paul says, 'Likewise the Spirit helps us in our weakness; for we do not know how to pray as we ought, but the Spirit himself intercedes for us with sighs too deep for words.' It is not too easy to give this a detailed explanation, but the implication seems to be clear. It is that prayer is not a matter of our trying, unaided, to offer something which will be acceptable to God. In a strange sort of way Paul is saying that God even helps us to pray to Him. The point of presenting this verse for consideration here is that its emphasis is strongly divergent from much of our approach to worship today. The Church is rightly very concerned to review her liturgies. When she does so, considerations of clarity, accuracy, order and relevance are naturally high on the list of priorities. And congregations, more than ever before conscious of high standards of public performance because of television, ought to be equally critical of anything which lacks clarity, coherence and order. In such an era, and welcoming each of these developments, it is good to be reminded again that in worship the 'standard of public performance' is not the most important consideration. There is the matter of worship being pleasing to God, which, if John is anything to go by,[9] depends also upon spirituality and truth. We may expect the Holy Spirit to guide our preparation of orders of Service and to aid us as we seek for the very highest standards, but we must also remember that, when we have done all, we still need His aid that our worship may be inward and true. And we can expect it; a fact which should cause us to relax a little more about our worship, and to concentrate upon the spirit as well as the form.

In addition to His work for the deepening of our faith, however, the Holy Spirit also works for the expression of our faith. The New Testament has quite a lot to say about how faith will express itself, and again we find the Holy Spirit the key to the matter. For example, He is the one through whom God in Christ gives gifts to the Church (see I Cor. 12 and Eph. 4). Some gifts would seem to be largely a matter of quickening and directing of natural abilities (which are, of course, themselves

---

[9] 'But the hour is coming, and now is, when the true worshippers will worship the Father in spirit and in truth, for such the Father seeks to worship him' (John 4:23).

God's gifts anyway). Others seem to be more supernatural in content, yet also God's gifts. The Charismatic Movement across the denominations is reminding us, as the Pentecostal churches have sought to do throughout this century, of the wide variety of gifts that the Spirit gives, and of the immense release they afford across the whole area of the Christian's experience. It is often in services of worship that people claim, and receive, such gifts. Since the Church is a charismatic community that is not too surprising.

One simply wishes to ask two questions at this point about the implication of this for our services. First, have not our services really given the impression that by and large there are very few gifts of the Spirit shared by our church people, and that mostly they are concentrated upon ministers, preachers, and choirs? One writer has spoken of the Catholic, Protestant and Pentecostal traditions of worship as 'altar centred, pulpit centred and pew centred'. Each reflects the place where the gifts of the Spirit are. Must we not move further in the direction of involving far more of our congregation in the actual conduct of worship? Secondly, one would wish to ask whether, quite apart from the leadership of our services, our congregations are ever made aware of the gifts of the Spirit for them, and encouraged to believe that He will give His gifts to them? The early disciples were effective partly because they knew themselves to be the recipients of 'power and authority' to do God's will in the world. When did we last attend a service of worship which sent us out feeling convinced about that for ourselves? It is the sense of receiving and exercising gifts in the Christian community at worship which underlines the fact that the gifts are to upbuild the Church and unify it.

But the Holy Spirit also produces what Paul calls His 'fruit'. Paul lists the fruit of the Spirit—'love, joy, peace, patience, kindness, goodness, faithfulness, gentleness, self-control' (Gal. 5:22–23). Two contrasts with the gifts are immediately apparent as one studies the fruit of the Spirit. The first is that while the gifts are abilities the fruit are qualities of character. The first are connected with what we do, the second with what we are. Churches have so easily become characterized by concentration upon one or the other. Those which have 'majored' on the gifts have so easily become eccentric, unreliable and lacking in the stability of Christian character. Those who have gone for character have equally easily slipped into sheer moralism and ineffectiveness. The gifts have so much about them of excitement, activity, achievement: the fruit is so concerned with quality, consistency, being. And we need both; therefore our worship should reflect and reveal both, as well as commending them. The growth in genuine Christian character which is empowered for service should be the aim of every church, and its worship should be evidence of it.

The second contrast is that while each Christian is not expected to have all the gifts, every Christian is expected to show all the fruit. For the fruit is really a description of mature Christian character, each item strengthening and balancing the rest, and all together producing a Christlike quality. The fruit is the setting in which the gifts are placed, and each gift needs all the fruit if it is to be properly grounded. This makes the task of steady, disciplined character-building a major priority in worship; and this requires both careful planning and regular worship. The goal is expressed by Paul in a most moving way. 'And we all, with unveiled face, beholding the glory of the Lord, are being changed into his likeness from one degree of glory to another; for this comes from the Lord who is the Spirit' (II Cor. 3:18). Whatever complexities this verse contains, one thing is clear, namely that as we concentrate our attention upon Jesus we become more and more like Him, and that the transformation which takes place is by the operation of spiritual power in our lives. We are engaged in a character pilgrimage towards Christlikeness.

This examination of the place of the Holy Spirit in worship prompts one or two final comments. The first is that it would seem, on the basis of the biblical material, impossible to conceive properly of the Person and Work of the Holy Spirit without accepting the reality of what one might call the supernatural. Without this element, the (so-called) work of the Spirit becomes in fact a description of human activity and response, a chain of cause and effect which does not require any connotation of divine activity at all. The second comment would be that the conflict between prescribed and extempore forms of worship becomes a secondary consideration which may in the end have more to do with background and temperament than with spiritual realities. What is important is that the freedom and order so characteristic of the Spirit's presence should not be hindered. Lastly, one may be justified in feeling how shallow many of our experimental services are (as are many of our traditional ones), and how much deeper we have to go in understanding the place of the Holy Spirit in worship before we shall get more satisfactory services as the rule.[10]

[10] This chapter largely ignores the work of the Holy Spirit in relation to the Sacraments and to the World outside the Church because these topics are more conveniently dealt with in Chapters 7 and 8.

Chapter Four

I AM

'I HAVE been crucified with Christ; it is no longer I who live, but Christ who lives in me; and the life I now live in the flesh I live by faith in the Son of God, who loved me and gave himself for me' (Gal. 2:20). Without attempting a detailed exposition of that verse one can see that here, as in many other New Testament passages, a very intimate relationship between the individual self and Christ is being described. What is striking about such verses is that they are portraying a *relationship* between two beings, a communion, rather than an absorption of the one into the other.[1] We shall be asking in this chapter a number of questions about this 'selfhood' and its relationship to God in Christ by the Holy Spirit, with particular reference to our worship.

We begin with the matter of identity, of the question, 'Who am I?' John Wesley records in his journal for Sunday, 8th February 1736, his interview with the Moravian leader August Gottlieb Spangenberg. Wesley's concern was with his Christian life. Spangenberg's first question was, 'Do you know yourself?' Wesley gave an affirmative answer, but was not too sure of its accuracy. He had certainly spent many years seeking to be clear about himself. In that sense the answer was true. But he did not find spiritual release until he learned, in the matter of salvation, to 'give himself away'. It was two years later when, having had a stormy time as a missionary, having returned to England and, above all, having been taught by another Moravian, Peter Böhler, the uselessness of self-trust, John Wesley became sure that he trusted Christ, 'Christ alone for salvation'. In one sense he learned about himself most clearly once he had given himself over. One recognizes in this situation the fulfilment of some words of Jesus, 'If any man would come after me, let him deny

[1] See A. R. George, *Communion with God in the New Testament*, Epworth 1953.

himself and take up his cross and follow me. For whoever would save his life will lose it; and whoever loses his life for my sake and the gospel's will save it' (Matt. 16:24–25; Mark 8:34–35; see Luke 14:27).

It is for this reason that the approach of this book seems to fly in the face of much modern thinking about religion. It is common nowadays to affirm that the major question is not, 'Who is God?', but 'Who am I?'.[2] One does not wish to deny that for many modern people that is the major issue where meaning and identity are concerned. Over against this, however, there is good Christian ground for asserting that man will only begin to understand the answer to the question of his own identity when he is placed in relationship to God, in whose plan of things alone will he find his proper identity. One's starting point in the tasks of evangelism or apologetics may often therefore be with questions of an existential character, but the Christian's attempt to understand himself will be much more closely related to a proper understanding of God. In that growing knowledge we find ourselves. And precisely for this reason the question 'Who am I?', is a proper one to raise in the context of worship. For the same reason it is right to ask the question after one has spent some time on the being of God, Father, Son and Holy Spirit. The 'Lord's Prayer', an ever-present element in our worship, is itself a pattern of right priorities in this matter. Christian worship ought in fact to be a constant reiteration of the truth that I shall only discover 'Who I am' as I explore more fully 'Who God is'.

Of course some degree of self-awareness is a necessary preliminary to any meaningful worship. We were created as beings distinct from God and are meant to relate to Him personally. For this a vital prerequisite is to be aware of oneself. But the point at issue in worship, as in the whole of the Christian life, is the offering of that 'self' of which I am aware; an offering which, as Jesus said, leads somehow to an ever firmer selfhood and a deepening awareness of what that selfhood is all about.

[2] David Jenkins gives a most helpful outline of this approach in Chapter Three of his book *Guide to the Debate about God* (Lutterworth 1966). The chapter is entitled 'Bultmann and the "But" of Faith'. Jenkins shows how Bultmann distinguishes between empirical experience and existential experience in favour of the latter. Then follow the words, '*The* question of existence is "What is it like for me to be me and what does it mean for me to be me?"' (pp. 60–1).

George Matheson captured this spirit with tantalizing clarity in
the successive verses of the hymn which begins:

> 'Make me a captive, Lord,
> And then I shall be free;
> Force me to render up my sword,
> And I shall conqueror be.
> I sink in life's alarms
> When by myself I stand;
> Imprison me within Thine arms,
> And strong shall be my hand.'

M.H.B. 596

Paul indicates something of the implication of this process in
some verses which are full of the language of worship and
sacrifice. In his letter to the Romans, at the end of a long
doctrinal and historical outline, Paul begins to turn to the
practical matters of daily Christian behaviour. The section
begins with the powerful exhortation, 'I appeal to you therefore,
brethren, by the mercies of God, to present your bodies as a
living sacrifice, holy and acceptable to God, which is your
spiritual worship' (Rom. 12:1). This verse has a wider purview
than worship alone, yet its language and principle are very
closely related to worship. Its implications are therefore very
relevant to our present theme.

There is first of all the concept of 'offering'. The Revised
Standard Version uses the word 'present'. Two aspects of its
usage are important. The first is that, culled from the language
of worship, it conjures up the picture of the careful response of
the worshipper. One has only to recall the scrupulous care
involved in Israel's worship; the detail about the nature of the
offering, its cleanliness, the appropriate time, place and person,
to capture some of the atmosphere of the word. It describes a
decisive, premeditated, serious act of offering. There is nothing
slipshod or haphazard about the activity it describes. And,
secondly, it is an offering as a response, not an initiative. The
offering is the human response to the divine initiative; the
'mercies of God' to which Paul refers in this verse are described
in the previous chapters, especially the first eight in which he
has outlined the entire plan of salvation in Christ. It is because
of all that God in His mercy has done in Christ, and through the

Holy Spirit, to set man free, that we should make the decisive presentation of ourselves to Him.

We reach here an extension of the point made in chapter two concerning the historical rootage of our faith in Christ. There the emphasis was upon the firm foundation it provides for our faith. Here we must stress that this activity in Christ is significant not only because it provides a basis for faith, but also because it reveals something about the God with whom we are dealing. In Christ we see not only a series of events which encourage us to speak of a 'way of salvation'. In Him we also see a series of events which are mirrors reflecting the being of God.[3] Jesus is what He is precisely because God is like that.

The activity of Jesus Christ therefore constitutes the basis of our relationship with God. In Him God both reveals what He is like and also extends His invitation to us[4] and lays His claim upon us.[5] Thus the careful spelling out of the gospel in the first eight chapters of Romans is the laying of the foundation on which God's offer is based and His claim made. Like the ministry of Jesus, the recounting of the gospel message is not intended simply to interest observers and hearers: it is meant to produce the crisis of decision, to create the possibility of response, to lead men to God. The 'mercies' of God invite and claim the self-offering of man. Do we expect our worship to be like that?

The contrast between the above words and our worship, which they are intended to describe, is painfully evident on so many occasions. In many services there is not even a proper reminder of what God's mercies are; His historical acts of salvation are neglected, or 'assumed', with the result that we are not properly conscious of having anything to respond to. As a

[3] Is this why, in John's gospel, Jesus is represented as stressing the close link between Himself and the Father, a link which His opponents consistently sought to deny? (See for example, John 5:19–46; 6:41–65; 7:14–21; 8:34–59.) Paul also shows concern to emphasize that the deeds of Jesus Christ are God's acts among men—Romans 5:1–11; I Corinthians 1:18–25; II Corinthians 5:16–21; Galatians 1:3–4; and Colossians 1:15–20.

[4] In the Synoptic Gospels the invitation is to enter the Kingdom; in John to possess eternal life, in Acts and the Epistles to respond to the gospel proclamation by joining the company of the believers via repentance, faith and baptism.

[5] There is a sense in which the claim and the offer are like two sides of the one coin. Our response to God's offer of salvation is the giving of ourselves—in this sense His offer is a claim. His claim upon us includes acceptance of responsibility for us—in this sense His claim is an offer.

consequence our worship lacks the urgency of offering as a decisive, premeditated, free act of grateful response. Where, on the other hand, the liturgy contains a regular recital of God's 'saving deeds', they are too often viewed as part of the necessary diet of worship, rather than the recital of divine activity by which the whole of world history has been given a new context. Failure to see this naturally precludes the whole-hearted response Paul enjoins upon his readers. In other words, it is not the inclusion or exclusion of a recital of God's saving acts and the verbalizing of an appropriate response which is the problem (though plainly their inclusion is more likely to produce the right worship). It is our failure to appreciate the importance of God's saving activity, and the need for total response, which lies at the heart of malaise in worship. And this failure is encouraged by careless preparation and leading of worship on the one hand: and by inadequate teaching ministry from the pulpit on the other. It would be a good test at our next act of worship to examine how far we are made aware of 'the mercies of God' (in terms of His provision of salvation), and what opportunity we have to respond in an urgent, decisive and meaningful way. Those of us who preach and conduct worship might test our preparation and content by the same standard.

Next we note the fact that Paul calls for the presenting of 'your bodies'. As a number of works this century have shown, this word is not casually chosen. It avoids the pejorative implications of a word like 'flesh', which usually stands for man's susceptibility to temptation and consequent rebellion against God. But it also steers clear of the word 'spirit', which normally implies man's capacity for and enjoyment of God's presence and will. Each of these words is a description, not of part of a man, but of man in his totality, seen from different points of view.[6] The word translated 'body' also refers to man in his totality, but avoiding pejorative or eulogistic overtones; it means the whole of a man, in his potential, one way or another, including the physical outworking of inner attitudes. The New English Bible renders 'your bodies' as 'your very selves'. Put another way, it means that provision is made within the concept for a man's works to express his faith (an idea sometimes wrongly associated only with James), for a man's life-style to

[6] See J. A. T. Robinson, *The Body*, S.C.M. 1957.

reflect his basic convictions, and for the whole of him to be involved in response to God's mercies.

Each of us may reflect on whether the worship he normally attends makes provision for this very demanding interpretation of our 'offering' of ourselves. Does the worship provide for the adequate physical movement, for example? Or is our part largely to sit still while one person does all the moving? And the repetition of standing, sitting and kneeling is hardly a remedy! The writer remembers one large congregation singing with great gusto (and melody!), the Battle Hymn of the Republic', chorus and all, but standing perfectly still as they did so! It seemed quite incredible that they should not themselves march around the church! But supposing the preacher had suggested it!

There is another question mark at the heart of our worship and preaching if we take this part of Romans seriously. Is the content of ideas, descriptions, exhortations and commitments sufficiently 'grounded' in the stuff of life? In other words, when I am at worship does it become abundantly evident to me what I must do tomorrow if I am properly to respond to what I am saying, singing, praying and hearing today? Or has worship become a sharing ground for middle-class religious theory of an academic kind? Are we stimulated both to thought and action by what goes on in church? Do we leave feeling that relationships have got to be repaired, specific relationships; that duties have got to be shouldered, particular duties; that new ventures in mission and evangelism must be begun, in particular places and ways?

Or we may apply the point the other way round. Since 'body' includes mind, am I mentally stimulated by the worship, or could I have left my intellectual apparatus behind since I can get through the monotonous repetition of our worship without thought?

Here we may recall the claim of T. R. Glover[7] that the early Christians, amongst other things, 'out-thought' their contemporaries. Few would wish to suggest that Christians today are not thinking people. In some ways the obstacles we face—allied

---

[7] *The Jesus of History*, S.C.M. 1917—'If I may invent or adapt three words, the Christian "out-lived" the pagan, "out-died" the pagan, and "out-thought" him' (p. 213).

to our often depressing statistics—give us too much to think about. There is plenty of thought, and there is a rich diversity of thought. Yet 'thought in worship' focuses our attention upon a serious problem for Christians. Three quotations, from writers of varied ecclesiastical and theological stand-points, introduce the nature of our task.

'There is no longer a Christian mind. There is still, of course, a Christian ethic, a Christian practice, and a Christian spirituality. As a moral being, the modern Christian subscribes to a code other than that of the non-Christian. As a member of the Church, he undertakes obligations and observations ignored by the non-Christian. As a spiritual being, in prayer and meditation, he strives to cultivate a dimension of life unexplored by the non-Christian. But as a *thinking* being, the modern Christian has succumbed to secularization. He accepts religion—its morality, its worship, its spiritual culture; but he rejects the religious view of life, the view which sets all earthly issues within the context of the eternal, the view which relates all human problems—social, political, cultural—to the doctrinal foundations of the Christian Faith, the view which sees all things here below in terms of God's supremacy and earth's transitoriness, in terms of Heaven and Hell.'[8]

'The original apostolic witness remains permanently at the centre of the life of the Church in order to provide the norm by which all subsequent development is judged and by which aberrations are corrected. There must be development. It is impossible simply to go on repeating the original words. They have—in the first place—to be translated, and all translation changes meaning. They have, then, to be re-interpreted to meet new situations. It is precisely by the vigour and courage with which the work of re-interpretation is done that the claim to finality is made good in the actual course of human history. Only when the Church has the boldness to re-interpret the original testimony in the face of new human situations is it able to make plain and effective the claim to finality. Re-interpretation always carries risks, but to evade risks always means to court disaster.'[9]

'The history of the church has been tarnished by a recurrent

[8] H. Blamires, *The Christian Mind*, S.P.C.K. 1963, pp. 3–4.
[9] Lesslie Newbigin, *The Finality of Christ*, S.C.M. 1969, pp. 77–8.

failure to hold together the oldness and the newness of the Christian faith. Sometimes it has successfully maintained the old faith, but failed to relate it to the new world. At other times it has been determined to communicate with the new world, but failed in the process to preserve the old faith in its purity. We have considered how what is old must be ever freshly appropriated and applied; we must now emphasize the need, while striving to speak relevantly to modern man, to remain loyal to the old, the original, the apostolic faith.'[10]

The reader may feel compelled to choose which—if any—of these expresses his view on this matter. But however he chooses he can hardly miss the issue raised by all three—how does the modern Christian remain faithful to the abiding truth of the Christian gospel and at the same time translate, interpret, respond to and proclaim it in a way which is authentic and appropriate in the (late) twentieth century?

It is here that the challenge to the mind in our worship is highlighted. If we do celebrate the 'mercies of God', His revelation of Himself in Christ, and His offer of salvation through Christ, how do these relate to the modern life as we know it, with its potential and its problems, its excitement and its boredom, its confidence and its self-doubt? We shall look at aspects of this question later in this chapter. Here it is more important to enquire whether our worship in any way makes us aware of this healthy tension, of this need for thought, of this challenge to mental effort and clarity in facing the problem. One fears that—as the writers quoted above indicate—we find it easier to resolve the tension by opting exclusively for the first century or the twentieth, rather than by facing the Christian task of properly relating the two. Because modern life is so varied and complex this responsibility of working out the relationship between the gospel and modern life must not be left to a select band of intellectuals.[11] It is for each Christian and all Christians to be part of this mental pilgrimage, of which our worship will be a focal point. Are our minds genuinely stimulated this way in worship as we know it?

[10] J. R. W. Stott, *Christ the Controversialist*, Tyndale Press 1970, p. 40.

[11] For a fascinating account of what this kind of challenge involved for Indian Christians who sought to translate their Christian faith against the background of their indigenous culture, see Lesslie Newbigin, *The Household of God*, S.C.M. 1955, p. 17.

Even intellectual stimulus will not fulfil all the requirements of the word 'body', nor meet all our needs as worshippers. We must also consider our involvement as people with the ability to make decisions, to affirm allegiance, to plan a course of action. In other words we are people with a will. This is not to introduce a frenetic note of constant crisis into our Christian experience in general and worship in particular. There is about much valid Christianity a calm and fixed obedience and service which constant crisis would weaken. Yet in a situation where we are citizens both of an earthly and a heavenly kingdom, where we live in a culture which is no longer pronouncedly Christian, and where the complexity of modern living demands a variety of decisions every day, it would be strange if one's Christian commitment did not involve frequent re-assessment of one's pattern of life, scale of values, list of priorities, stewardship of time, talents and money. And this will often result in new decisions, or the reinforcing of old ones, as the implications of being a Christian are borne in upon us. Moreover, if our worship is the focal point of our offering to God, and an important time for seeing life as under God, it is proper to expect such re-assessment and such willing response to take place when we meet as a worshipping community. The intensity may not be that described by Isaiah in the temple (Isa. 6:1-8); but the principle is surely the same. To be particularly aware of God's presence is to see life as it is before Him and to seek to play our part in making it what He wishes it to be. And that will require a willing obedience.

Why should we not also be moved emotionally in worship? Our emotions are part of our bodies. Have we, as Martin Thornton claims, become so afraid of feelings in religion that we deprive ourselves and others of the fullness available to believers? We are rightly concerned about intellectual integrity and vigour, and about persevering and determined discipleship. Ought we not to be equally aware of the need for emotional experience and expression in worship? The Charismatic Movement and some of our predominantly young people's groups may teach us something about this.[12] Many of our brothers and sisters in Christ from overseas could certainly do so. The stolid Anglo-Saxon phlegm we display in much of our

[12] See, for example, the recent 'Come Together' experiments in worship.

worship must leave them wondering about us! Why should we not be deeply moved at the story of the birth of Jesus; or weep at the story of Judas, or burst out into songs of praise on resurrection day? We would be strange creatures indeed if the mercies of God did not so move us. But are we to inhibit freedom of emotional expression in His house of all places? How can we present our bodies with bottled-up emotions?

A positive response to each of the questions presented by the paragraphs above, and an eager expectancy on our part that it should be so, might well revolutionize much of our worship. It would cease to be merely 'something we do'. It could become a time of total involvement, of wholehearted worship, of presenting our bodies. It is not a plea for 'gimmicks', nor for 'audience manipulation'. It is a vision of groups of Christians who are 'free to be' in the presence of God and of one another; who, in their awareness of all His mercies, present their whole selves afresh to Him as liberated people who gladly serve Him. This, in turn, might have a liberating effect upon our tenseness (often) in relationships in daily life.

Thirdly, we need to give due consideration to the word translated 'spiritual' in the Revised Standard Version. It will also bear the rendering 'logical', 'rational' or 'reasonable'. Whichever one chooses, however (and scholars vary in their preference), there is common to each the concept of inner compulsion based on conviction. The earlier use of the word 'body' should not blind us to the fact that the response called for has its human source in a man's inner being: it is not the automatic, externally programmed performance of the machine. It has to do with the deep inner wells of a man's being, touched by the stimulus of the gospel and its significance, flowing over in torrents of grateful response as like speaks to like. And it is precisely in that attitude of overflowing response that I begin to discover 'who I am'. It is then that, like Abram at Ur, Moses in the desert, Isaiah in the temple, Matthew at the seat of custom, Paul on the Damascus Road, I begin to perceive my true destiny as it is placed against the background of God's over-arching sovereignty; I become aware of the reality of my being as I know it in relation to the being of God. I am not owner, but owned; not creator but creature; not discoverer but the recipient of revelation; not master but steward. Yet, by the very same token, and in the very same relationship, I am not bound but free; life is not meaningless but purposeful; the road does not narrow but broadens; I am not robbed of self-hood but rather find it enhanced and enlarged. I am who I am because He is who He is, and I perceive and enter into this reality as I see the former in the light of the latter.

We must now try to put all this into more positive and practical terms by means of a number of assertions about our worship. We shall use as our guide another part of scripture appropriately related to worship, namely the Psalms. Passages are chosen arbitrarily as representing typical insights into the nature of man and God.

First, our worship should affirm man's role in the world. In Psalm 8:5–6 the writer spells it out in well-known words:

'Yet thou hast made him (man) little less than God,
  and dost crown him with glory and honour.
Thou hast given him dominion over the works of thy hands. . . .'

Here again the 'am' of man's existence is placed alongside a consideration of God—'O Lord, our Lord, how majestic is thy name in all the earth!' (Ps. 8:1). Yet the overall effect is not to belittle man but to elevate him. The Psalmist is able both to assert the majesty of God and to stress the glory, honour and dominion of man. On the whole the Christian church has found it very difficult to follow the Psalmist in retaining this right balance. We have either belittled man in order that God might have the praise believed to be His due, or we have so highly assessed man's 'coming of age' that we discover by the same process that God has died![13] And it would not be too difficult to show that our worship is much affected by im-balance in either direction—the reluctance to acknowledge genuine human strength and achievement on the one hand, and

---

[13] The intriguingly close connection between these two was highlighted by Dr David Pailin's reminder that many of the 'Death of God' theologians were origin-ally followers of Karl Barth. In Barthian theology man's extreme limitations are stressed, over against the sovereign freedom of God. In the 'death of God' theology that freedom was extended to include the right to 'die on us'. 'The "Word" is held to be so sovereignly free that it can proclaim the "death" of the "God" of any of its former expressions! The Barthian assertion of the utter freedom of the "Word" over against the human bondage of natural theology is thus extended to cover the possibility of negations of previous revelations'—(David A. Pailin, *The London Quarterly and Holborn Review*, October 1967, p. 276).

the (more recent) almost total concentration upon man's potential and duties (the 'When I needed a neighbour were you there?' syndrome). The Psalmist refuses to make such a choice.

We may go further and say that he could not make the choice, for the simple reason that each part of what he asserts depends to some extent upon the other. Part of the majesty of God is expressed in His bestowal upon man of such power and dominion: man, on the other hand, is at his most masterful peak precisely as he accepts his role as God's steward. He will develop the world, rather than exploiting it, as he finds his place in God's plan for the world. He will share its resources, rather than greedily keeping them for himself, as he recognizes that all God's gifts are for all His creatures. He will develop his enormous potential most confidently as he realizes that the ultimate control is not in his hands but God's. At the same time God's majesty is the more clearly seen as the world is developed, its resources shared, man's potential realized, for it all takes place against the backcloth of His creative purpose. Each part of the Psalmist's statement needs the other if it is to be fully meaningful. And so does our worship.

We may sum up this point as follows: the corollary of the majesty of God is not the weakness of man but his potential strength, while the outcome of every new step of man's development is intended to be a fresh awareness of the greatness of God. But how is our worship to celebrate this basic fact of man's identity? In the first place it is clear that our prayers of thanksgiving need to take account of what has happened in our modern world. Much of our praise is still couched in the pastoral setting of the Psalmist and, for that matter, earlier ages of Christianity in England. Hills, valleys, seas, fields, skies somehow seem to have more poetry about them than factories, computers, blast-offs (or blasts-off) and satellite communication systems. Yet it is the latter which provide the setting for most of our living, and unless we feel it the Christian duty to restore our land to its former rural condition we must learn to praise God in technological terms too. God, after all, made man capable of this kind of development, exactly as He made him able to till the land. If we are grateful for the opportunity to 'plough the fields and scatter the good seed on the land' then we must also thank God for the ability to 'focus scientific pressure on clouds to make them give rain'.

Nor must we be grudging about man's achievements, in the 'scientists can do this, but . . .' manner. If we are true to our Psalmist we may gladly affirm every discovery of the potentiality of the universe in which we live. The power to explore space, investigate the sources of life, provide for and organize more leisure time, is all God-given power. In our worship we ought not to be slow to acknowledge and celebrate the fact.

Yet, and this we must also say in response to the Psalmist, it remains *delegated* power. Man's greatness is that of the steward handling his master's goods, the servant exploring the possessions of his lord. And this means that man's potential has a purpose about it, a purpose against which all that he actually achieves will have to be measured. In other words, the assertion of man's delegated power places alongside the question, 'Is it possible?' another question 'Is it right?'. It is here that our earlier chapters begin again to have relevance. We need our dimensions, our points of reference, our focus on Jesus Christ as the clue to living, our awareness of and obedience to the leading of the Holy Spirit. And we shall find ourselves constantly affirming thankfully man's God-given potential, while in the same breath confessing with shame the wrong uses to which it is sometimes put. This means that worship will be a process of affirmation and confrontation; we affirm thankfully man's dominion under God, and we and our world are confronted by God's being and by His purposes for His world. One might almost say that our position in the world is brought under weekly corporate review! And within this process I discover more of what it means to say, 'I am'.

This question of values by which we assess man's performance in the world leads us naturally to an entirely different emphasis (one might even say 'mood') of the Psalmist. By contrast with the buoyant affirmatives of Psalm 8 we turn to the groping heart-searchings of Psalm 42:1-2. 'As a hart longs for flowing streams, so longs my soul for thee, O God. My soul thirsts for God, for the living God.' The mood is very different, yet the two have a close connection in relation to our topic. It is all too easy for Christians either to belittle man in order to glorify God, or to elevate man at the expense of God. But if one wishes to take both God's sovereignty and man's potential and performance seriously, then agony is unavoidable, for one is faced with a whole range of perplexing questions. 'Where do I draw the line between right and wrong?' 'How far am I to interfere with natural processes?' 'Where does my scientific investigation become a threat to human freedom?' 'Who is to decide, and by what criteria, what is permissible?' And, above all, 'Where am I to find genuine personal satisfaction in this whole process of living in the world with all its excitements and perplexities?' If God and the modern world are taken seriously these questions have got to be faced.

The Psalmist, though not facing those particular questions, had his own set of problems, for him equally perplexing and agonizing. His response to them is, in the manner of the good builder, to drill down to bed-rock. Personal inner experience of the living God will alone satisfy him, an experience based on hope which is in turn fed by the knowledge of what this God has done and will do. This personal relationship, as we should put it, is for him basic. And it is a conscious relationship, something felt and reflected upon—the relationship one enjoys with those one lives with, rather than with the policeman whom one never meets though he affords protection to one. I discover the identity of 'I who am' as I am in living relationship with 'He who is'. It is precisely at this point that words fail adequately to describe the reality. Even the Psalmist talks about 'deep calling to deep' in an attempt to communicate something about it. It is deep and it is real; it is decisive and it is personal—and so one could go on. It is the meeting of a man with his God; and this is bed-rock for genuine Christianity. As the other questions are related to this one they begin to have a proper position in the scale of things.

Without this relationship modern man is like the driver of a high-powered car without any idea of the route to take. The machine is full of potential and he knows how to drive it. But without precise insights into the proper direction he may move off along a road which steadily takes him further and further from his intended destination. In this situation he may from time to time both admire and service the engine, praise the comfort and attractiveness of the interior, even be the envy of others who see him speeding by. But the fact is that built-in

frustration of his position is made the more intense by the very
speed, capability and efficiency of the vehicle. The Psalmist
had his own problems without the guidance of God; modern
man has his. The life-style and ethos of each is extremely
different from the other. But each needs a personal relationship
with God if life is to be truly meaningful. The manner of this
awareness of God, this divine self-disclosure, this inward source
of satisfaction, has been variously described. But despite the
variety of description it remains part of the essence of the truly
religious experience.

Thus one finds oneself asking a question which seems so
unnecessary, and yet which may well lie at the heart of many of
our current expressions of unease about worship. 'Do we expect,
any more, to encounter the living God in our worship?' To use
modern jargon, 'Does the area of our expectancy include a
divine/human encounter?' Whom do we expect to meet at
church? As we all reach for our dictionaries, or begin to talk
about empirical verification, or even start our reply with 'It all
depends what you mean by . . .', one is inclined to say, somewhat harshly no doubt, 'You know what I mean!' Are we aware
of Him as we worship?

This is not to raise here the question of whether we meet God
only in church. One doubts whether any Christian in any age
has ever believed such a thing. We are not at this moment
concerned with what happens out of worship, but with what
happens *in* worship. Nor is one debating the issue of modern
spirituality being exactly the same as in previous ages, or
entirely different. (In passing one might comment that it is
difficult to see how it could be either.) Nor is the assumption
here that everyone will be aware of God's presence in the same
way. What is basic to this section, however, is that worship
must have at its heart a personal encounter with the living God,
and that without this it will not satisfy.

With this in mind we may offer two comments about the
practice of worship in many of our churches. The first is to ask
whether, in any of our denominations, prospective worshippers
spend sufficient, if any, time preparing themselves for worship.
It is after all to be a meeting with the living God! This is not a
matter of enjoining silence on a congregation at a specified time
before worship begins. One has sat in churches without any

sense that it was being used for preparation for worship. It is rather a plea that we should all see the need *for* preparation in readiness for such a momentous weekly event.

The second comment is offered, notwithstanding what is written above, as a request for more silence during our times of worship. The inability of our culture to handle silence is well known. So is the long experience of the Church that in silence God is sometimes particularly perceived. It is also in silence that I may, albeit in the presence of my Christian brothers and sisters, offer to God those very personal experiences which make my life mine and not anyone else's. It may well be that neither the liturgy nor the preaching has in a particular service made me aware of what it is to be me at this particular moment, simply because nothing said or done relates to my particular experience at present. In the silence the specific context of my life can be offered and His presence known. And the presence of other Christians does matter, for we share the fellowship of silence together.

A third perspective on worship is still needed from the Psalmist, however. Worship rightly affirms man's role in the world. It also properly involves a meeting with the living God. In each of these I am discovering what it means to be me. Yet each of these steps assumes that I have both the right and the ability so to relate to God. Neither the biblical teaching as a whole nor the gospel in particular give us much ground for such an assumption. In both there is considerable awareness of unworthiness, inability and hopelessness on man's part. If contact is to be established, it must come from 'the other side', if we may use a spatial metaphor without being misunderstood. So the Psalmist, in Psalm 103:3–4, encourages himself to praise God, 'who forgives all your iniquity, who heals all your diseases, who redeems your life from the Pit, who crowns you with steadfast love and mercy . . .'. Forgiveness, healing, longevity, love, mercy and renewal are all included in the list referred to as 'his benefits'. The recalling of the benefits is the basis of the thanksgiving. Without the benefits no thanksgiving would be possible, for the benefits include the enabling which results in thanksgiving.

This brings us back to a recurring theme in this book, namely the priority of divine grace which makes worship possible at all. The Psalmist lists some of his experiences of this grace: we could list many more. Like Paul in Romans we can catalogue the whole sweep of gospel events and their individual, communal and cosmic significance.[14] In this way we see what a great privilege it is to participate in worship. In days when church attendance has been on the decline there is a tendency to treat worship as an act which helps the Church out. It becomes a way of 'voting with our feet' for God. In such circumstances we easily lose our sense of privilege. The reminder that we approach God in worship is a reminder that we do so only because He has made it possible and welcomes us. And the ground over which we approach Him is the ground of the gospel—God's continuous, forgiving, redeeming, enabling love, supremely revealed in the life, death and resurrection of Jesus Christ. The recognition and acceptance of such privilege is a vital part of understanding what it means to be me.

We may sum up thus far by reminding ourselves that I begin to discover what it means to be me as I see myself in relation to God's being. This is disclosed to me through 'his mercies', His saving acts in Christ, made real by the Holy Spirit in my life. My response is a careful, decisive offering of myself, every part and faculty, inspired by the inner conviction of His grace. In responding I find my place in the world affirmed; God's majesty places me in a role of dominion, albeit a delegated dominion. In this position I am most totally free when most bound to His will, most completely myself when giving myself to Him. I also discover that, at the bottom of all the search for meaning, there is my need for a personal relationship with God, deep to deep. And the whole basis of such worship is God's benefits which inspire the worship, and God's mercy which enables it. I am what I am because He is what He is. The more worship reflects this truth the more wholly satisfying it will be, and the more worthy of Him. In all of this the presence of my fellow Christians is vital. To this we must now turn.

---

[14] See, e.g. Romans 1–8, ending in the triumphant assertions of 8:31–39.

Chapter Five

WITH THEM

'Sanctified in Christ Jesus, called to be saints together with all those who in every place call on the name of our Lord Jesus Christ, both their Lord and ours' (I Cor. 1:2). Paul's opening greeting to the Church at Corinth, though traditional, is full of interest. For example, the words 'sanctified' and 'saints' come from the same root. They have already been 'set apart' by their faith relationship to Christ, signified in their baptism; now they are called upon to become what that implies, presumably in every part of their lives. This is often expressed in terms of 'become what you are'. For our purposes the most significant feature of this verse is that they are called to be saints 'together with all those who in every place call on the name of our Lord Jesus Christ, both their Lord and ours'. When one recalls how prone the Corinthians were to emphasize the importance of particular Church leaders (I Cor. 1:10–15; 3:1–9), particular groups of people (I Cor. 11:17–22), and particular types of spiritual gift (I Cor. 12–14), this corporate emphasis of Paul takes on still greater significance. Part of the trouble threatening the life of the Church at Corinth was the inability of some of its members properly to balance the 'I am' and the 'with them' of the Christian life. To express it in terms of this book, they were willing to explore their personal identities in relation to God, but not so willing to do so in relation to other Christians. Paul appears to be suggesting that their failure in the latter relationship casts doubt upon their sincerity and authenticity in the former.[1]

Becoming a Christian must be a matter of individual and personal commitment. No one can finally commit me; I must

[1] This would seem to be the meaning of I Corinthians 11:17–34, where their wilful neglect of one another is taken as a sign of their failure to eat and drink 'worthily' (v. 27); or to 'discern the body' (v. 29), which brings judgement upon them (v. 27–32).

commit myself; and I cannot commit anyone else. There is an essential inwardness and integrity at the heart of the Christian experience which can only be safeguarded by the personal individual right to choose or to reject. True worship must be 'in spirit and in truth' (John 4:24). There is an inwardness and sincerity required which cannot be coerced. Even so, the presence and influence of others in relation to that commitment it patently obvious. Many of us who are committed Christians were baptized as infants—we did not achieve that by ourselves; indeed in some cases the service was probably carried through in spite of our noisy protestations! We were received by the community of faith which baptized us. The faith of that community provided the setting of response to gospel promises in which our baptism took place. We were trained at home, at school, at Sunday School and Church. We observed the lives of those who professed to be Christians. In fact a large number of individuals, and a number of communities made it possible for us to be increasingly, or suddenly, committed to God in Christ in our own personal, individual faith response.

Even those who were not privileged to have a Christian upbringing share with those who were so privileged the common value of the very existence of the Church as the community of God's people. No Christian would wish to deny the many failures of institutional Christianity. Nor can we ignore the fact that many must have been hindered in their search for faith by the weaknesses and faithlessness of Christian groups. Nevertheless the fact remains that it is precisely within the corporate life of the Church that the gospel has been preserved, understood, expounded and received. Its own sense of being unworthy and yet continuing as the people of God is a testimony to the gospel which brought it into being and by which it must be constantly tested. The complex and varied debate about faith and tradition[2] in the life of the Church is itself a testimony to the value of a continuity of organized groups of believers.

It is even more clear that however individual *becoming* a Christian may seem to be, *being* a Christian can never be a purely individual affair. Under normal conditions of life there

[2] For two examples of this discussion see F. F. Bruce, *Tradition Old and New*, Paternoster 1970, and Gerhard Ebeling, *The Word of God and Tradition*, Collins 1968.

is no such thing as an isolated Christian. To belong to Christ is to belong to His people. To be committed to God is to be part of His family. To possess the Holy Spirit is to be linked by the Spirit to all others who are possessed by Him. One of the reasons for corporate worship is to celebrate the family nature of the people of God. Alongside the I-Thou relationship of man and God there is the I-They relationship of man to fellow-men. So integral is this to Christian worship that we need to explore both its theological foundations and its necessary expressions in our worship.

This is not the place for any lengthy theological discussion, but one can feel the weight placed upon corporateness in the biblical tradition by referring to some basic concepts.

As with so many other Christian doctrines, the starting point is to be found in the Hebrew thought and expression of the Old Testament. Israel begins with the call of one man, Abram (Gen. 12). God deals henceforth with a family and a nation, within which prophets, priests, kings and other individuals find and express their place. The pilgrim people who set out on their journey from Egypt to the Promised Land are terrifyingly dependent upon one another, as well as upon God; as various incidents reveal. Above all, as the nation develops, the chosen leader represents the whole people very strikingly. The fact of their being in the Covenant (Gen. 15, 17) and 'under the Law' (Ex. 24), serves to strengthen their oneness. Above all there is the fascinating, and at times perplexing, interchange between individuals and groups. Jacob is an individual, yet often the word Jacob means the people of Israel. The servant of Isaiah 53 seems also to possess individual and corporate personality. This bewildering interchange of single and group identity is not a matter of careless thought or expression. It reflects a very deep factor of human living as a whole—our interdependence in life—and a basic concept in Israel's awareness of God. They were His people—a corporate entity within which true identity as individuals was meant to be discovered, preserved and enjoyed.

One might expect New Testament teaching to move away from such a concept, since the people of God are now to belong to any nation, and are not constituted by birth and culture. And to some extent this does happen. The teaching of Jesus introduced an element of crisis and decision for each individual who heard Him. He even said that response to Him would break up the normal units of Jewish society—family, synagogue, city (Luke 12:51–53; 21:12; 13:34–35). Moreover He consistently sought out individuals—especially outcasts—and received individuals who sought Him, as though to emphasize the importance of the individual over against the group; the significance of personal choices over against the deadening uniformity imposed by the machinery of the institution. In many ways the individual came into his own in the presence of Jesus.

Nevertheless, the corporate element remains strongly present: the more strongly as individuals find a proper liberation within the company of the people of God. One of the most significant aspects of Jesus' earthly ministry was the gathering around Him of a mutually dependent group for instruction, training and fellowship. Between Christ's Ascension and the Day of Pentecost a larger group of His followers continued their devotional life together (Acts 1:12–14). After the events of Pentecost they were joined by the new converts in an even more clearly recognizable and compact group, committed to certain fixed religious activities, and providing mutual support by the pooling of resources (Acts 2:41–47). Even when that stage of development ceased, the emphasis upon the corporate nature of the faith was retained by such metaphors as 'the body of Christ',[3] 'the temple of God',[4] 'the bride of Christ',[5] and so on.[6] In each of these cases, and a number of others, a singular verb is used to describe all the Christians, and in each case the reason for

---

[3] Corinthians 12, especially v. 27; Ephesians 1:23 (where Christ is the head of the body), 4:12; Colossians 1:18 (where the usage is like that in Eph. 1:23), 1:24 (Ephesians 5:30 and Romans 12:5 are slightly more oblique references). For discussion of the exact significance of this expression see J. A. T. Robinson, *The Body—A Study in Pauline Theology*, S.C.M. 1952, and Ernest Best, *One Body in Christ*, S.P.C.K. 1955. For an application of this teaching to the life of the church see Alan Cole, *The Body of Christ—A New Testament Image of the Church*, Hodder and Stoughton 1964.

[4] I Corinthians 3:16–17; II Corinthians 6:16 (I Corinthians 6:19 uses a similar image, but applies it to the individual bodies of the group addressed).

[5] II Corinthians 11:2; Ephesians 5:25–27, 32; Revelation 19:7; 21:2; 22:17. For Old Testament basis for such usage see Isaiah 54:6; Jeremiah 2:2, 3:20; Ezekial 16:8; 23:4; Hosea 2:16.

[6] For treatment of these and many other images of the Church see Paul S. Minear, *Images of the Church in the New Testament*, Lutterworth 1961.

their oneness is indicated by the link with one or other members of the Trinity.

The two gospel sacraments emphasize the same point.[7] Baptism—perhaps particularly infant baptism—stresses the community aspect of the Christian faith, as the child is brought under the Covenant, received into the family of the Church, and assured of training and example towards his own personal commitment to Christ later. In the same way the Lord's Supper is essentially a corporate experience. We share the one loaf and the one cup, symbols of our oneness in redemption. Other aspects of our church life, such as the concept of membership (commitment to belonging and to responsibility) or stewardship (the pledging of time, talent and money in the service of God through the church), underline the same basic principle: we belong not only to Him, but in Him to one another also.

Corporate worship is meant to be a celebration of this truth week by week. It is the gathering together in each place of the members of Christ's body, the reconstituting of the temple of the Holy Spirit, the family gathering of the people of God. Thus together we share the gospel sacraments, hear the gospel word, and reaffirm our membership of the Church and the stewardship of our lives. In theory it sounds remarkably simple and obvious. But what are its implications, and how far does the reality live up to the theory?

We begin with the observation that worship is not meant to be isolated from life as a whole. The prophets in the Old Testament inveighed against their fellows precisely because their everyday life was not in harmony with their worship (Isa. 1:12–17; Jer. 7:1–7; Amos 8; Mic. 6:6–8). In the temple they affirmed the qualities of mercy, justice, righteousness; in their business life their actions denied these very attributes. In the New Testament there are similar criticisms. The words of Jesus about putting a wrong relationship right before making an offering to God are in the same vein (Matt. 5:23–24). So is Paul's condemnation of the Corinthian Church, where the rich arrived early at the agape meal and were surfeited with food and drink by the time the hungry, thirsty slave believers arrived to find nothing left (I Cor. 11:17–22).

[7] See Chapter Seven for fuller treatment.

4

One group went into the Lord's Supper overfed; the other underfed. Paul's major criticism of such unfair distribution is that it denies the oneness and harmony of the body of Christ. Their behaviour outside worship could not simply be 'forgotten' or made 'unimportant', by what they did in worship. Each was intended to be in an harmonious relationship with the other.

Now it is at this precise point that the relationship of the individual believer to the group in worship is most seriously threatened. Our 'nuclear' society, as it has been called, with its divisions into small nuclear family units (many living almost anonymously in relation to their neighbours and each fiercely defending its autonomy in decisions about its life), does not aid the sense of oneness of Christians at worship. And many of our churches have settled into this ethos all too successfully. There is no area in which to meet people before or after worship. There is no time for coffee before or after worship when one might get to know people. The pews effectively cut us off from all except those who sit on our left or right. We get out at the end with a handshake. How much have we felt the oneness of the body of Christ? In any case how could one feel it when fifty to a hundred are scattered across a church built to seat two thousand? In such cases our worship is conforming to the isolationism of life outside, instead of daily life becoming more like the warmhearted openness to one another of Christian fellowship.

These problems are not easily solved, but they certainly will not be until we recapture the sense of belonging to one another which is meant to characterize God's people. It must, of course, be pointed out that the physical circumstances of those who expressed this oneness in Old Testament and New Testament were very different from ours. Both the isolated chosen people of Israel and the small self-conscious Christian church were a compact group because of the variety of threats from without. (Perhaps the best modern illustrations of such circumstances came from the black churches in U.S.A. ghettoes, or the underground churches of Eastern Europe.) But such conditions, and the difference in ours, should not blind us to the deeper reasons for their oneness, whatever the setting in which it was expressed.

They were aware of oneness because God has constituted

them His people. As Peter so eloquently reminds his readers, in words reminiscent of Hosea: 'Once you were no people but now you are God's people; once you had not received mercy but now you have received mercy' (I Pet. 2:10). They belonged to one another because, by God's sovereign activity, they had been brought into the company of His people, each of them and all of them. Their attitudes and actions were meant to express that position, as a faith response to what God had done for them. They were part of the *one* people.

Or again, they were aware of their oneness because they were part of the Body of Christ. Paul's extended metaphor on the body (I Cor. 12) is well known. Each Christian belongs to each other Christian, and is dependent upon and responsible to each other Christian, as a hand is to an eye, a foot to an ear. The breaking of the oneness between Christians is as serious as that. The most striking expression of this basic unity occurs in verse 12 of this chapter. Paul writes, 'For just as the body is one and has many members, and all the members of the body, though many, are one body, so it is with . . .'. It would be an interesting exercise for each reader to put in the word or words which follow. Logically it should be 'the Church'; the ending of the sentence reading 'So it is with the Church'. This is the drift of the whole argument. But in fact Paul ends the sentence with, 'Christ'; 'so it is with Christ'. He means 'the Church', but he wishes to convey unforgettably the ground of the unity and oneness of the Church; it is none other than Christ Himself. (This is why, towards the beginning of his first letter to Corinth, when chiding the readers for their divisions over different leaders, Paul asks crushingly, 'Is Christ divided? Was Paul crucified for you? Or were you baptized into the name of Paul?' (I Cor. 1:13). The answer is obviously, 'No!') The oneness of Christians stems from the oneness of Christ Himself. They are part of the *one* body.

And they are possessed by the one Spirit. Paul links this with the 'body' analogy. 'For by one Spirit we were all baptized into one body—Jews or Greeks, slaves or free—and all were made to drink of one Spirit' (I Cor. 12:13). We shall look at some of the implications of this later in the chapter. Here we simply note that the Spirit who indwells each believer, who gives gifts to God's people, who makes Christ a reality to them, is *one*

Spirit, part of whose work in the world is to unite God's people. They are part of the temple of God, built by the Spirit on the foundation of Jesus Christ.

Now all of the foregoing might be passed off as purely academic information, the manipulation of theological counters. And so it could easily be. But not if it is in fact describing a reality, *the* reality at the heart of the universe—the unity of the triune God. Diverse in operation yet totally in harmony; revealed in law and prophets, in flesh and blood, in Spirit and power, yet always in a unity of intention, of action, of love. The doctrine of the Trinity affirms this oneness at the heart of life's original, continuing and ultimate reality. And to belong to God, to be open to and possessed by that reality, is not only to glimpse the musical score of the divine symphony, it is to join the earthly orchestra whose privilege it is to play the melody, however limited, with earthly instruments. The unity of God is expressed in the oneness of Christians!

It therefore does matter that we should take steps to get to know better those with whom we worship; to get to know them better during the week that we may more consciously express our oneness at worship. It really does matter to know our fellow-worshippers, so that the prayers offered may not only have meaning when my particular hopes or needs are included, but also when hopes and needs of my brothers and sisters around me are incorporated. It really does matter—how trivial it sounds—to sit together in church for worship, and not be scattered about the building like the bones of a disintegrated skeleton, dry and disconnected. And it really does matter that I should be 'in love and charity with my neighbour'; that resentments and quarrels be settled before worship begins. All of this—and much more that follows from it—matters, not because it will make our worship more satisfying (though it will), but because only then will our worship truly represent things as they are, with God and with His Church as He intends it to be. The unity of the Godhead is the ground and pattern of the oneness of each congregation of God's people, the body of Christ, the temple of the Holy Spirit—and of all His people. Our worship should be a constant reminder and expression of that fundamental link which stands as a constant challenge to all Christians, in every congregation.

In such a setting, and with such a basis, the worship I offer will be less and less concerned solely with myself. I shall seek in my worship-encounter with God not only to understand myself better, but also to understand everyone else better. How much of our assessment of worship *is* self-centred. *I* didn't know any of the hymns; *I* didn't follow the readings; none of the prayers gripped *me*; the preacher didn't speak to *my* need; or even (may we be forgiven), *I* didn't get *my* regular seat! Of course the individual matters in worship; and individual encounters with the reality of God are at the heart of our worship; but so is the reality of the community at worship. How we need to gain the deeper sense of the 'we', as well as the 'I', at worship!

We have thought about 'oneness'. We need also to explore the corporateness of worship in terms of 'fellowship'. Strictly speaking, fellowship simply means 'going shares with'. There is the fellowship of the rugger club, the Women's Institute, the farmers' association. It is not the sharing, but 'what is shared' that is distinctive (though what is shared will influence the nature and quality of the sharing. I'd rather belong to a fellowship of voluntary social workers than a fellowship of hired assassins, for example!). The main characteristic of Christian fellowship is meant to be that it is Christian. This means that I share with others the knowledge of God, in Christ, by the power of the Holy Spirit. It also means that I share with others the privileges and responsibilities which go with that knowledge; privileges and responsibilities which are expressed in my life in and out of church. And because of the nature of that which is shared, there is added to the fellowship the deep quality that none of us who so shares even begins to deserve what he has in common with the others. It is a sharing which is entirely dependent upon God's grace.

Therefore we must ask to what extent our worship expresses such fellowship. Put in that form the question is capable of answers along two different lines. One is to describe the fellowship experienced outside our formal worship, which is expressed within our worship because we are the more closely linked together. Thus a congregation which meets in fellowship groups during the week to share together insights, convictions, experiences, problems, aspirations, service, as Christians, is

more likely to enjoy a rich fellowship at Sunday worship (just
as a person accustomed to praying daily at home is more likely
to be able to follow and participate in the prayers in church).
We need to look very carefully to discover whether the cause
of the dryness and emptiness and individualism of much of our
corporate worship does not in fact spring from our lack of
fellowship *outside* formal worship. The sad truth is that for many
Christians the only time the name of Jesus crosses their lips
seems to be when the singing of a hymn requires it (or the
simple questioning of children in the home embarrassingly
raises the point). If we get so little practice, or have so little
desire in the matter of speaking together about what is supposed
to be the central passion of our lives, no wonder our worship
lacks fire!

But there is another line of answer to the question about
fellowship. This is to ask how far our formal acts of worship
give the opportunity for fellowship. Of course we (mostly) try
to do things together. We sing together, say responses (perhaps)
together. Mostly, for the rest, we *listen* together. It is what
Eugene Brand calls, 'spectator worship'. He points out that
even the seating arrangement in churches is more akin to
'audience seats' than 'player benches'.[8] No wonder it is difficult
to 'get in on the action'. The architecture suggests that we are
really there to 'watch the pro' perform.

Doubtless it is difficult in large congregations (though not
impossible, as Pentecostal worship has been demonstrating
throughout this century)[9] for a high degree of individual
participation in public worship. But many of our churches are
certainly small enough for a much larger amount of sharing to
take place. If we believe that the Spirit preserves and deepens
our unity by the gifts He gives, then worship should provide
for the engagement of those gifts for the benefit of all and to the
praise of God. This is not the place for blueprints: but it is the

[8] Eugene Brand, *The Rite Thing*, Augsburg 1970, p. 20.

[9] 'The Pentecostal church meeting has been described as pew-centred, and the
description is apt. In contrast to generally pulpit-centred Protestantism and altar-
centred Catholicism, Pentecostalism finds its centre in the believing community'—
Frederick Dale Bruner, *A Theology of the Holy Spirit*, Hodder and Stoughton 1971,
p. 132. He quotes one Pentecostal writer who states that, 'we never reach the point
where our congregations are composed of on-looking spectators rather than
participating worshippers'. This contrasts strikingly with Brand's criticisms
(above) of worship as he knows it.

opportunity for all responsible for worship to ask whether we really care to have the congregation truly sharing, to the full, in the worship we seek to lead. And it does not have to be participation by speaking. There are many forms of human expression, as we shall suggest in a later chapter. It is the concern that it should be so which matters at this point; and the desire of congregations to be cast less in the role of spectators and more of genuine participants.

One must go a little further to say that behind such a concern there needs to be some theological conviction. Worship has often become a spectator activity because of the view of the ordained ministry and its place within the Church. As long as the minister is viewed as the 'professional Christian' who 'works for the church', while all others are viewed as 'amateur Christians' who 'go to the church' there will be a tendency towards spectator worship while the amateurs watch the professional doing all that really matters. Both the view that the ordained man is within himself a different person because of ordination, and the view which sees him purely in functional terms will tend to reinforce this kind of practice. In the former case there is often the feeling that things are somehow better if done by him, in the latter it is, after all, what he is paid for anyway. Midway between these two is the concept of the ordained minister as a representative person; representing within his position and office that which the Church is; but not operating exclusively within that role, rather existing to enable others properly to fulfil that role alongside him without detraction from his own distinctive position. It is easy to see how this interpretation of ministry could also lead to a situation in which we leave it all to our representative, but only if the concept is misunderstood. A recovery of clarity about the doctrine and office of the ministry as representative would improve this aspect of our worship enormously.[10] Otherwise we may have more and more spectator worship. Or we may—

[10] For a full discussion of the meaning of the ordained ministry and its relationship to the Church see K. E. Kirk (ed.), *The Apostolic Ministry,* Hodder and Stoughton 1946; Stephen Neill (ed.), *The Ministry of the Church,* 1947; T. W. Manson *The Church's Ministry,* Hodder and Stoughton 1948; T. W. Manson, *Ministry and Priesthood: Christ's and Ours,* Epworth 1958; A. T. Hanson, *The Pioneer Church,* S.C.M. 1961; John Stacey, *About the Ministry,* Epworth 1967; Clive Porthouse (ed.), *Ministry in the Seventies,* Falcon Books 1970; Hans Kung, *Why Priests?,* Fontana 1972.

by way of revolt—have types of worship which detract from
the proper role of the ordained minister.

Related to this question of ministry and laity in worship is the
currently topical issue of the gifts of the Spirit and their exercise
in worship. The use of lay men and women in conduct of
worship and as preachers is a traditional way in many churches
of acknowledging and using the Spirit's gifts in worship.
Pentecostalism however, and more recently the Charismatic
Movement, have introduced afresh the question of the whole
range of gifts mentioned in the New Testament as coming from
the Holy Spirit;[11] including the phenomenon known as singing
in the Spirit. There are two sides to this question. One concerns
an examination in detail of each gift and the nature of its
reception and use in public worship. To this the 'charismatic'
Christians themselves are giving some attention. Apart from this
detailed examination, however, there remains the more general
question of freedom to exercise—in public worship—the gifts
of the Spirit. The problem had to be faced in first-century
Corinth, as Paul's first letter to the Corinthians shows. It has
to be faced by the contemporary Church in a slightly different
form in that each denomination has a well-established tradition
of worship, incorporated into various orders of service. Many
of these seem to be threatened by the 'charismatic' approach to
worship. In some places the result has been a split in the
congregation, followed by secession. In other cases the 'charis-
matics' enjoy their distinctive forms of worship in mid-week
meetings, thus avoiding a clash of interests but also losing the
opportunity to share their insights and experiences with fellow
Christians in the context of public worship.

It is easy to pronounce on this subject by excluding one
element or other—planned order or spontaneous order;
presumably both inspired by the Holy Spirit—but to do so is to

[11] There are now many books on this phenomenon. The following, on both sides
of the discussion, are typical. Michael Harper, *Walk in the Spirit*, Hodder and
Stoughton 1960; Morton T. Kelsey, *Tongue Speaking—an experiment in spiritual
experience*, Hodder and Stoughton 1968; James D. G. Dunn, *Baptism in the Holy
Spirit*, S.C.M. 1970; Dennis J. Bennett, *Nine o'clock in the Morning*, Coverdale 1971;
F. Dale Bruner, *A Theology of the Holy Spirit*, Hodder and Stoughton 1971; Donald
Bridge and David Phypers, *Spiritual gifts and the church*, Inter-Varsity Press 1973;
William R. Davies and Ross Peart, *The Charismatic Movement and Methodism*,
Methodist Home Mission Occasional Paper, 1973; Roger Salisbury, *The Holy
Spirit Experience*, Lutterworth 1973.

eliminate a tension which has constantly recurred in the life of the Church and has protected her from lifeless predictability on one side and spontaneous triviality on the other. A life-giving solution is surely more likely to result from an attempt by those who influence patterns of worship denominationally and those who make decisions about forms of worship locally to discover points at which the two traditions—of fixed liturgical worship and spontaneous worship—properly meet and might be shared to the mutual enrichment of each. The welcome given to the Charismatic Movement in some of the major denominations ought surely to encourage this kind of pioneering work amongst us.[12]

'Oneness' and 'fellowship'. There is a third criterion for examining the relationship of each individual worshipper to his fellow worshippers; the criterion of 'distinctiveness'. There is a bond between Christian believers because they are 'different'. Since this is not so popular a Christian concept today we need to look at it with some care. It is not raised here as though to assert that God is only at work within the confines of the Church. Neither is it to suggest that the Christians are in any sense different in their own right from other men. Nor that Christians cannot learn much from others. But it is to assert that Christians—those who have responded to God in Christ—are, for that reason, possessors of distinctive privileges and responsibilities, by reason of which there is a closer bond between them than between any of them and those who are not so privileged or responsible.

The New Testament word *ekklēsia*, translated 'church', really underlines this point. It refers to those who are called out. One New Testament word for preacher, *kērux*, the herald (I Tim. 2:7; II Tim. 1:11), points in the same direction, since the herald declared a fixed message to the citizens, inviting, for example, to the meeting of the assembly. Those who responded constituted the assembly. The *ekklēsia* are those who responded to the gospel message (called *kērugma*) of the herald and constitute the gospel assembly. We see the same distinctiveness in the description of the Christians in Acts as belonging to 'the

[12] Statements from Roman Catholic, Presbyterian Church of Scotland and British Methodist sources have all given a welcome, with certain reservations and suggestions.

Way' (Acts 19:9, 23; 22:4; 24:14, 22; see also 16:17 and
18:25f.); as living in such a way that those who joined by
repentance, faith and baptism knew that they had joined a
distinctive group, and the rest dared not do so (Acts 5:13). The
picture of the Church as a 'pilgrim people (I Pet. 2:11), the
designation of Christians as 'saints' (Acts 9:13; Rom. 12:13;
I Cor. 1:2; II Cor. 8:4; Eph. 1:15; Phil. 4:21, etc.), people set
apart for God, the description of them as 'a chosen race', 'a
royal priesthood', 'a holy nation' (I Pet. 1:9) all point in this
direction.

But the purpose of this calling is meant to destroy the possibility of those attitudes and positions which modern critics
of the distinctiveness of the Church—critics from within and
without—wish to avoid. The Church is the distinctive people
called to show what God intends for everyone, and has the
responsibility not only to proclaim God's will but also to
exemplify it. There should be no 'elitism' here, no 'triumph-
alism'; only a deep sense of wonder at the grace of God and a
humble obedience to the will of God. And it is important that
this aspect of the life of the Church should be expressed,
because it is only as she sees herself in her properly distinctive
light that she fulfils her task as she ought. Otherwise she spends
her days blurring the edges between herself and others; loses
that proper distinctiveness which is God's gift and not her
right; and ceases properly to rely upon divine power in fulfilling
her task.

Our worship therefore needs to emphasize the fact that by
God's grace we are privileged and responsible. As I recognize
my place in that people, and my part in that task, I cease to be
an individualist, concerned with my own salvation only. I
become a participant in the life of the total community of God,
and a worker in His world, to fulfil His will, 'till the earth is
full of the glory of God as the waters cover the sea'. Thus both
the nature and the intention of the triune God will be in process
of working out through the people of God in the world.

Chapter Six

AROUND THE BIBLE

From time to time in previous chapters a certain assumption
has been made without any attempt to defend it. This is that
the Bible is basic to our understanding of worship. To this we
must now turn.

This is not the place to explore in detail the origin, compila-
tion and nature of the Bible. There are very many books on
each of these subjects. But it is the place to raise questions
about the relationship of the Bible to our worship. We may do
this in two ways. There is first of all the information and insight
it affords us concerning worship in the earliest Christian
communities. In this way we can discover something about the
worship which was offered shortly after the ministry of Christ.
Then there is, secondly, the question of how we use the Bible
in worship today. Ought it to be as central to our contemporary
services as traditionally it has been? If so, do we make the best
possible use of it?

We begin with the evidence it supplies of how the earliest
Christians worshipped. Here the material is not extensive but
it is important. There is, for example, some *description*; 'they
devoted themselves to prayer' (Acts 1:14). One assumes that
this would be in addition to normal attendance at the temple,
as Acts 3:1 suggests.

The reasons for this emphasis are not too difficult to discern.
They were, after all, Jews, and their Scriptures contained many
stirring accounts of how their spiritual heroes had spoken to God
and listened to God in prayer. Added to this was the example of
Jesus Christ Himself. Each new development in His ministry
seemed to be preceded by prayer. He had taught His disciples
the importance of prayer in their spiritual development, and
He had taught them how to pray. The lessons so learned had
borne fruit when, on the Day of Pentecost, the company who
had 'devoted themselves to prayer', received the gift of the
Holy Spirit (Acts 2).

In prayer they reaffirmed their dependence upon God.
Perhaps this is why our modern world finds prayer more
difficult. We have such capabilities ourselves, and we wield
such power, that dependence on some unseen force seems less
necessary, or even less defensible. Yet if God is the Creator, then
even the materials and energy by which man 'comes of age' are
a gift from God. We only push our dependence one stage further
back, and in so doing we reveal how basic it is. If God, by
definition, is the source of all created matter then we may only
abolish our dependence by abolishing God. Grant His existence
—as God the original Creator—and dependence is inevitable.
In prayer we recognize this inevitability, and affirm it, at
whatever level.[1]

But prayer was privilege also. As they prayed they affirmed
and experienced their dependence: but they also claimed their
rights, as Jesus had taught them to do. One of the basic
assumptions behind Christ's teaching on prayer was that God
was their heavenly father, and a father is known to act in certain
ways when his child makes requests. The way of prayer, therefore, need not be a limiting path to adopt, though it has been so
when men have chosen to pray *instead of* working to solve the
problem rather than *in addition* to doing so. The way of petition-
ary prayer both acknowledges man's dependent state as an
inevitable reality and affirms his greatest potential and freedom
in co-operation with God his maker. This is not to limit but to
extend man's actual power, and to give him a greater dignity
as a co-worker with God (Eph. 2:10).

The New Testament picture of prayer[2] is a much wider one
than that, however. Petition is really a secondary, though
important feature, as the Lord's Prayer shows.[3] There is an
integrity and dignity about Christian prayer because its first
concern is with God. 'Our Father who art in heaven' is an
exploration of who He is, the first half stressing His loving

[1] For three different treatments of the subject of prayer, see O. Hallesby,
Prayer, Inter-Varsity Press 1948; Mark Gibbard, *Why Pray?* S.C.M. 1970; I. T.
Ramsey, *Our Understanding of Prayer*, S.P.C.K. 1971 (Archbishops' Commission on
Christian Doctrine, Occasional Paper No. 1).

[2] For a commentary on New Testament prayers, see Donald Coggan, *The
Prayers of the New Testament*, S.P.C.K. 1967.

[3] For a brief but penetrating commentary on the Lord's Prayer, see D. Martyn
Lloyd-Jones, *Studies in the Sermon on the Mount*, Inter-Varsity Press 1960, Vol. 2,
Ch. IV–VI, pp. 45–77.

nearness; the second half His transcendent otherness. The next section of the prayer concerns God's purposes—His name to be hallowed, His kingdom to come, His will to be done. As yet there is no mention of the needs of the one who prays. He is taken up with God's nature and will. Only then does he offer requests for himself—and others. *Our* daily bread; *our* trespasses; lead *us* not into temptation. Seen in this light prayer is in fact a rehearsal of the Christian life, its concern to know God's nature more fully; to understand and play a part in realizing His will; and to enjoy that relationship with Him in which life is full because it finds its total meaning and expression in His will.

One might be pardoned for doubting whether such presuppositions inform our corporate prayer these days. It seems so often to be a rather tired recitation of well-known formalities —whether set or extempore—without much communal vigour or life. It is there, like flowers without root which may be seen lying in a garden—visible but without life or hope of it; there largely because a garden is where flowers should be. The biblical descriptions of prayer challenge us to look beneath our practices to our reasons, beyond our words to our motives, beyond our appearances to our intentions. In this way we may become aware of prayer as an exploration and affirmation of the realities of our existence, and as an electrifying encounter with the One whose being lies at the heart of these realities.

In Acts 2:42 there is a rather fuller description, however, and a more significant one in view of the already rapid growth of the Church. There are now four characteristics picked out. The 'apostles' teaching' we take to be indicated by the outlines given in Acts, in particular the relating of Old Testament passages to the events of Christ's total ministry.[4] It is interesting to observe the priority of the teaching function at this point.

Again it is relevant to our consideration of worship. For the early Church, the realities of existence which they expressed in worship now contained two new elements. One was the realization that their Jewish history was not an end in itself, as the chosen people had tended to think, but was merely a preparation for something greater, as some of their prophets had hinted, but without being listened to, and indeed without

[4] For an examination of the way in which Christ Himself did this, see R. T. France, *Jesus and the Old Testament*, Tyndale Press, 1971.

fully grasping the import of their own words. Now, however, the earliest Jewish Christians recognized the preliminary nature of their previous experience of God.

The second element follows directly from this, namely that Jesus Christ summed up in Himself all that God had been preparing for in the history of the Jews. Jesus Christ is seen both as the fulfiller of 'Old Testament' categories, and as the one who reveals their inadequacy as final explanations of God's will and way. He is the new wine which first fills and then bursts the old bottles. In this setting some clear explanation of what God had actually done in Christ was essential. This the apostles' teaching supplied, and the young church worked out the implications step by step, as passages like Acts 10, 11 and 15 show.

This historically rooted objectivity, this account of the mighty saving acts of God, remains crucial to our understanding too. This is one reason why, after our much experimental and free worship, and our loss of nerve about preaching, we are returning again to worship which contains the regular recitation of the drama of salvation, and to the need for an exposition of some part of that drama, by whatever means. Otherwise our worship becomes like the journey of a ship without a magnetic north; like a game without rules; like an orchestra without a score. The result is chaos, or a sense of pointlessness.

Here the apostles, who had witnessed the events of Jesus' Ministry and Resurrection (see their qualifications in Acts 1:21–22), provided this basis of teaching. We may assume— though it is no more than assumption—that the instruction they gave was the spoken basis of the later written documents which we call the gospels.

'Fellowship' simply means 'sharing together', 'going shares with'. Since breaking of bread is mentioned separately 'fellowship' cannot simply be a reference to the Lord's Supper. It may refer to the agape meal which seems to have been shared prior to the Lord's Supper (I Cor. 11:17ff.), But most of all it would seem to refer to the sharing together of their common life in Christ in their mutual attitudes (Phil. 2:1–4), their helping of one another (Gal. 6:1–6), their sharing of God-given gifts within the body of Christ (Rom. 12:3–8; I Cor. 12) and their seeking to build one another up in the faith (Eph. 4:1–16). What they shared together was their new-found experience of life in Christ.

Next comes 'The breaking of Bread'; an essentially simple meal which commemorated both the last supper of our Lord with His disciples and also His death which it represented. On this we must note two separate points. The first is that, if the records of the Last Supper in the gospels (Matt. 26, Mark 14, Luke 22, John 13) are taken as our guide, the Lord's Supper would have something of the form of Jewish table prayers. 'Simple' does not therefore necessarily mean 'informal'. The second is that the meal would have special associations for them, in that, during His earthly presence before and after the Resurrection, many significant happenings had been associated with meals which Jesus shared with His disciples. Quite apart from the detailed interpretations of the Lord's Supper, there-fore (of the kind attempted elsewhere in this book), the actual biblical *record* of the Supper draws attention to two main factors. One is that it was associated with the presence of Jesus —present to the spiritual apprehension of the participants, though not dependent upon it. The other is that it was essen-tially a corporate activity, even though the table conversation could easily individualize the occasion within the communal setting, as some accounts show. It was in the presence of their brethren that their individual apprehension of the meaning of the Supper was experienced. It was a presence of Christ *to them all*, within which it was a presence to *each of them*. Their individual awareness of Him required the setting of the group because the Supper was essentially a group experience. This is why Paul was so horrified to learn of the Corinthian practice of not even waiting for one another, so that some had too much and others too little. It is not without significance here that Paul goes straight from this point to write about the Church as the Body of Christ (I Cor. 11–12). The excessive individualism of the readers threatened the life of their church at a number of points, and the Lord's Supper was one. In passing we may wish to ask whether sufficient significance is attached to participa-tion in the Lord's Supper as an affirmation of the corporateness of the Christian faith, of our oneness with fellow believers, or whether it is not too concerned about how much we 'get out of it' as individuals. There is a healthy biblical emphasis upon

an objective reality—the oneness of the Church—in association
with the Lord's Supper. By adhering to it we avoid the difficulties, at present created by our unbalanced emphasis, for
those who by nature do not find symbolic actions or objects
particularly meaningful, and yet who affirm their oneness in
faith with other Christians.

Finally 'the prayers' which seems to suggest something rather
more formal than the 'prayer meeting', though there are
examples of these in the Acts too (see Acts 4:23–31; 16:25–34).
As Jews it seems likely that they brought with them into their
worship many of the traditional prayers which they had
learned, though now they understood them in terms of Jesus
Christ.

In particular we may note the strong emphasis in the New
Testament on the 'right of access' to God in prayer which is
available to all Christians (see Ch. 2, pp. 50–51). This is
reflected in passages where the Christian faith is being contrasted with others, such as in the letter to the Hebrews. Here,
in an argument contrasting Christianity with Judaism, the
writer contrasts the Jewish system—heavily dependent upon
the High Priest, the priests, the sacrifices and the temple—with
the Christian system, in which Christ is both High Priest and
Sacrifice, the temple is the presence of God Himself, the veil
next to the Holy of Holies is Christ's flesh broken for us, and in
Him each believer may freely approach God (Heb. 10:19–25).
It is not surprising that this letter contains a number of exhortations to come boldly to the 'throne of grace'. It is a
characteristic New Testament emphasis.

We are not limited to descriptive sections of the New
Testament, however, for our understanding of the worship of
the early church. We learn some things from passages of
exhortation. Thus we read of 'psalms, hymns and spiritual
songs' being used (Eph. 5:18–20; Col. 3:16), under the influence
of the Spirit, and in order to give thanks to God through Jesus
Christ. The parallel with drunkenness (Eph. 5:18) communi-
cates something of the mood of worship there involved: the
reference to 'the peace of Christ' ruling the heart, and the
'word of Christ' indwelling the believer, with an emphasis upon
'wisdom' (Col. 3:15–16) suggest that the joy was never intended
to be irresponsible or carefree, nor the inspiration of senseless

speech or behaviour. It may be of some significance to ask how far certain temperaments, nations or cultures lean naturally in one or other of the two directions outlined above; ecstatic joy and peaceful wisdom. One might go even further to enquire whether this is inevitable, or whether the highest Christian worship will find room for both in all its expressions.

In particular we in this country still have to solve the problem of national or age differences in our worship. Immigrants from parts of Africa and the West Indies are reported as judging our forms of worship to be lifeless, restrictive and too formalized. Others, from different traditions in Africa, or from Asia, often find us too shallow or pragmatic. The result is separate congregations along national lines, each able—as we say—to 'worship in its own way'. The problem is no more serious, but often strikes our congregations as more serious, when groups of young people break away from their churches to have services of their own which are more exciting, informal and lively— more geared to the modern 'scene'. It is here that the familiar biblical pictures of 'body' and 'family' become so relevant. In the body each part needs the other, not operating independently, by a kind of voluntary self-amputation, but actually linked to and serving one another, together. In the family all the members seek to arrive, together, at a common way of life within which the whole family expresses its oneness without the individuality (not individualism) of any of its members being unduly curtailed. Is the body of Christ and the family of God to be the only exception? Are charismatic and contemplative, traditional and modern, formal liturgist and free experimentalist doomed for ever to worship apart? Does variety inevitably produce unharmonious worship? Can that which each viewpoint seeks to safeguard not be protected—and even enhanced —while being placed alongside other viewpoints? Perhaps now that the first phase of the battle is over, experimentalist charge being met by traditionalist counter-charge, we may all sit near the battlefield to discuss whether underlying our different rallying cries there are not more important unifying presuppositions which we share with one another.

As well as description and paranesis there is also a *disciplinary* element in the New Testament, and here too we learn about worship. Thus we read Paul's restraining words to Christians

intoxicated with exciting spiritual gifts—especially the gift of
'tongues' (I Cor. 14). In this context some of the guiding
principles of worship emerge. 'Upbuilding', 'encouragement',
'consolation' and 'edification' (vv. 3–5) are highlighted in
connection with public utterances in the assembly. And the
prime condition for the above benefits is 'understanding'
(v.2). The intelligibility of what is spoken is a prior ground for
the understanding which is vital to proper education. The
context is the contrast between prophesying and speaking in
tongues without interpretation. It would perhaps apply better
in our day to different kinds of preaching, or a contrast between
various liturgies. The aim of intelligible speech which edifies is
two-fold. For the believer it is maturity of thought (v.20), for
the unbeliever it is conviction in the presence of God (vv. 24–25).
And the best context for this is one of decency and order, hence
first, the outline of a simple service; second, the restriction on
women participating vocally (bearing in mind the social setting
of the day and the gross misunderstanding and perhaps abuse
which could have resulted): and third, the acceptance of
apostolic discipline (vv. 26–40).

One must, of course, emphasize the fact that the manward
direction of the movement of worship is here under review, not
worship as a whole. But the simple test of our public utterances
in worship is a challenging one. Are they intelligible? Are they
calculated to meet the needs of the hearer—if a Christian to
lead him to mature faith?—if an unbeliever to lead him to
faith? In other words they have to do with a declaration and
explanation of the truth, properly applied to the hearers'
condition, rather than with displays of erudition, spirited
exhortations or entertaining performances. There may be more
truth than we wish to allow in the comment by Paul Althaus
that people are not tired of preaching, but tired of *our*
preaching.[5]

Recorded conversation provides another source of our understanding of early church worship, since we may presumably
conclude that they recorded what they believed to be important.
Thus we find words of Jesus about worship, in response to the
questions of the Samaritan woman at the well (John 4:19–26).

[5] Helmut Thielicke, *The Trouble with the Church*, Hodder and Stoughton 1966,
Translator's Note by John W. Doberstein, p. viii.

e to worship: His answer is about *how*
truth' (v. 23). In this context 'spiritual'
supernatural creativity, with the new
verflowing in worshipful activity of the
ruth' means genuineness and authenti-
contrasted with idolatry, because its
and its basis is God's revelation of
e pattern of obedience to God's will
us. Applied to our worship it affirms
words there must be an inner ex-
which relates to God's historic activity
od's saving work at a point in history,
r experience of that saving activity
, are meant to serve as the 'gold in the bank' which
provides a meaningful existence for the 'currency notes' of our
words and actions in worship.

There is also *visionary material*. In vision the man of God sees
the perfect worship of heaven, and records it (Rev. 7:9–12).
Here the emphasis is upon the unifying nature of worship.
Though many in number, various in tribe, race and language,
they are united in the manifold experience of worship. They
are in one location—'before the throne and before the Lamb'.
The implication here appears to be that the object of their
worship—the heavenly throne—and the one who has made
possible their journey here—the Lamb—focus their attention
and unite them in doing so. The first ground of unity is not our
desire to be united, nor our regard for one another, important
though both of these are. The primary ground of unity is
our common focal point, God who led us to Himself through
Christ.

Secondly, they are one in wearing white robes and waving
palms. The robes are taken to be symbols of resurrection life;
the palms of victory after war. This is the unity of common
experience—God-given experience, dependent upon Christ's
death and resurrection.

In the third place they are united by common ascription of
praise to God: the unity of purpose and motive.

The sum total of these comments on worship puts a question
mark against some of our contemporary attitudes to the subject.
Their worship and unity are focused upon God and His work;

the experience which unites them depends upon what He has done in Christ; the motivation and intention of their worship is to ascribe praise to God. How different it all appears from our anthropocentric concerns, our worship which seems almost wholly taken up with reflecting upon man and his plight, resources and duties. As Richard Wurmbrand, who suffered prison and torture for the faith, commented upon worship in Britain 'I miss the presence of the angels'. There are welcome signs that a renewed sense of the reality of God, the reliability of the gospel message and the authenticity of Christian experience is enabling a new awareness of God as the unifying and validating factor in worship.[6]

In one sense the most important point to derive from all this is how little actual detail is given and how informal it all appears to be; perhaps strangely at odds with much modern writing on worship, where details of content and order are emphasized. We need, however, to balance a number of considerations before reaching too firm a conclusion. The first is that the earliest Christians were mostly Jews, and that they appear to have carried into their Christianity much of their traditional Jewish worship. Records in Acts show them attending the temple and the synagogues, for example; certainly until increasing conflict produced a break (Acts 2:46; 3:1; 5:42; 9:2, 20; 14:1, etc.). We must not assume that they left behind the high degree of formality in worship on becoming Christians.

Secondly, however, we must also remember that Christianity rapidly spread beyond the confines of Judaism. The extension beyond the Jews of Jerusalem to Jews of the dispersion, to Samaritans and to Gentiles is a major motif in the Acts of the Apostles (see the 'marching orders' of Acts 1:8). As the gospel spread to different centres, midst a variety of cultural settings, both the form of worship and the problems connected with it appear to have been various. Perhaps we ought, from time to time, to look again at that mixture of decent order and charismatic freedom in the New Testament which appears to hold

[6] Among such signs one would include the growing interest in spirituality and centres of spirituality, both Catholic and Evangelical; the success of special gatherings for worship, like 'Come Together', and the increasing desire of Christians to share their faith with others.

together what we seem inevitably to separate—a separation facilitated by our denominational life.[7]

In different circumstances and at different times a whole variety of method and activity will be required. The balance between the elements will constantly change, too. But variety, freedom and spontaneity are much more to the fore. In days of liturgical renewal we need to take the distinction to heart lest we strangle our worship with the rigidity of our own systems. Equally we need to guard against the common tendency to claim a particular *pattern* of worship as 'biblical' (meaning that the pattern in detail and order is distinguishable in Scripture), *to the exclusion of any other pattern.* Beyond this there is the parallel tendency to be committed to a pattern or patterns of worship developed traditionally, patterns which are not contrary to Scripture, but then to argue from this tradition to the exclusion of other patterns developed in other traditions and equally consonant with biblical teaching.

Perhaps a greater problem today, however, is not the relation of our worship patterns to biblical teaching and the subject, but the second main topic to which we alluded at the beginning of the chapter, namely, the place of the Bible itself in worship. This is not simply the problem of time elapsing since biblical material was written. It is rather that the cultural setting has so radically changed. Almost every presupposition of the way of life of the first century appears to have been overthrown or vitally changed between then and the twentieth. Basic attitudes to the universe, history, health, education, morals, individual and community life all seem to be vastly different. Can information, teaching and interpretation of events from the first century have any normative value for the twentieth? A number of modern scholarly approaches to the Bible in our century have reflected the pressure put upon us by such a question.[8] An increasing tendency in some churches to read non-biblical literature instead of a lesson from the Bible, and of some churches to dispose more frequently with the sermon are

---

[7] See Ferdinand Hahn, *The Worship of the Early Church*, Fortress Press 1973, for a detailed account of these developments, and reflection upon contemporary worship in the light of them.

[8] James Barr, *The Bible in the Modern World*, S.C.M. 1973, is a good example. By contrast, however, see *The Bible Speaks Again*, S.C.M. 1969, a work produced by the Netherlands Reformed Church.

reflections of the uncertainty about the relevance and status of the Bible as far as worship is concerned.

A number of comments are called for at this point. The first is the very obvious one that a refusal to use a reasonably modern translation provides an unnecessary barrier to the hearers. The second is that to read large tracts of the Bible at a time to congregations who are accustomed to receive most of their information by word and picture is expecting too much of them. The third is that if the Bible is read and preached with conviction there is much more likelihood that its message will be taken seriously. The fourth is that people who read their Bibles throughout the week as a devotional practice are much better placed to understand and respond to the reading and preaching on a Sunday in worship.

Having said all this, however, we must still face the rather weightier problem of different cultural and thought patterns which divide us from the first century AD and earlier. How are we to cross this divide?

A basic clue to solving the problem is that we must first endeavour really to understand what any given biblical writer was actually trying to say. For this there is required of us a genuine attempt to exercise historical sensitivity. Our modern existentialist ethos makes us altogether too impatient with the past and its emphases or significance. One Christian contribution to such a situation is by our determining to take the past—since it belongs to God—seriously. Where the Bible is concerned this will mean seeking to understand the circumstances, occasion, writer, recipients and contents of any given passage. It will also involve an attempt on our part to place ourselves in his position and grasp what he was seeking to communicate. If we find this difficult it is often because we are so little practised in the art. Even sermons regularly use the text as a mere starting point. We need help to experience followship with biblical writers in seeking really to understand them.

This will lead naturally to something else—a distinction between principle and application in biblical material. Certain biblical material is a matter of principle—changeless and timeless. Other material is by way of application and is necessarily related to the actual circumstances prevailing at the time. The application of the same principles may be different in our setting. But we first locate the principles, rather than rejecting all the teaching because the applications do not appear to be revelant.[9] The way in which Bible readings are introduced in worship and the use of the Bible in preaching can make a great difference to our understanding at this point.

Thirdly we need to give weight to the idea of 'fullness of time' concerning the cultural setting of the Christ event. No doubt we were all taught at school how invaluable to Paul were the communications of the Roman Empire and the common language spoken. We should add to these both the readiness for a new religious insight and also the thought forms available at the time, from Jewish religion, Roman life and the Greek language. It may be that we must see through the thought forms and words to the truth contained in them, but the value of those very forms and words may not be laid aside because our culture finds them difficult or uncongenial. The great New Testament words associated with salvation are a case in point. We may wish to find new words to describe the truth involved, but our test of the adequacy of our words must be the content of the biblical word meanings.[10]

Next it is worth pointing out that the biblical material is almost all the detailed record we have of the great events at the heart of our salvation. Their inspiration does not depend upon this alone, but the events they describe give them a uniqueness we neglect at our cost. For this reason alone it is necessary that in each act of worship the Bible is read and pondered, so that the foundation of our faith and worship be not obscured by neglect or forgetfulness.

Especially we must notice at this point the difference between an event and its interpretation. This is not the place to enter into the very considerable discussion of the relationship between the two, and in particular of the point at which

[9] John B. Job (ed.), *Studying God's Word*, Inter-Varsity Press, provides a good illustration of such an approach to the Bible. As a specific use of the method see Ch. 8 of that book, entitled 'The Bible and Contemporary Issues' by Donald English.

[10] On the difficult subject of the death of Christ, see Leon Morris, *The Apostolic Preaching of the Cross*, Tyndale Press 1955 for an attempt to give proper weight to Biblical teaching in the contemporary setting. More recently Pauline Webb, *Salvation Today*, S.C.M. 1974, has made a similar approach to the subject of salvation beginning with biblical definitions and working out from there.

apparent descriptions of historical events actually become interpretation (see Ch. 2, p. 46). But assuming that, for example, the gospels do describe as an event the death of Jesus Christ, we still face the questions 'What does it mean?' and 'Where shall we discover what it means?'. If there are indications that this may be an event with significance beyond that normally attaching to human affairs then our questions are even more tantalizing. In the Bible, however, we find an account of this and other events, and an ascription of their origin to a source behind and beyond—as well as within—human agencies. If we begin to try this suggestion out as an hypothesis we discover that both in the events of Israel's history leading up to the 'Christ events', and in the subsequent history of the Christian Church, there are factors which are signposts to divine initiative being involved. Should we then seek to find an alternative interpretation of all these phenomena, as well as their relationship to everyday life, and to our own personalities and problems, we shall probably end up somewhat frustrated. But even if we admit—initially—some divine initiative we must still seek a meaning, which involves seeking some source containing a meaning. Here again the Bible writers make their claim. Jesus Christ is born; an event. But it means 'Emmanuel ... God with us'; for He is 'the exact representation of (God's) being'; He is 'the image of the invisible God' because 'in him all the fulness of God was pleased to dwell'. He is the eternal Word become flesh to dwell among us (Matt. 1:23; Heb. 1:3 (N.I.V.); Col. 1:15, 19; John 1:14). The same treatment is afforded His teaching, His deeds, His death, His resurrection, His departure and His gift of the Holy Spirit. If we abandon these interpretations we may well ask on what grounds we still accept the events. And we must face two further difficulties. One is that if our Christian doctrines are based upon the Scriptures (since there is little other factual foundation for them), then we must note that there is in Scripture a high doctrine of Scripture itself and of its inspiration. Can we legitimately accept the former and reject the latter? If, on the other hand, we reject Scripture as normative for our doctrine we must face the fact that Jesus is recorded in the gospels as giving the Old Testament Scriptures a very authoritative place in His own life, thought and teaching; and as making promises to His disciples which make a similar view of the New Testament not only intelligible but convincing.[11] If obedience to Christ is the hallmark of a Christian, do we have the right to omit it here?

Next we must note—though sadly without space for either an adequate statement of the case or a full answer—the objection to the normative place of the Bible based upon cultural grounds. Everything is now so different in the twentieth century that first-century (and earlier) considerations, however important, cannot be normative. Our environment, our values, our expertise and our knowledge (including knowledge of the Bible and its origin in its cultural setting, together with the use of methods of critical scholarship) preclude us from giving allegiance to a first-century book. The argument is an important one, and deserves full hearing and response. Here we might notice one distinction which is important; the distinction between nature and culture. That which is natural is what happens to us as humans: that which is cultural determines the shape in which our natural existence comes to us. To be born is a natural experience, common to all human beings: to be born in a modern clinic or a bush clearing is a cultural alternative. To eat is part of the natural: to eat with implements or with the hands is determined by cultural heritage. A Christian might say that sin is natural, though its cultural forms may vary greatly from time to time and place to place. One uses this last illustration to lead to the conclusion. The Bible is of course written in a cultural setting—or series of cultural settings—and the natural realities of which it speaks take cultural shape appropriate to their time. It is moreover, very important that all appropriate critical methods be used to discover the exact origin, purpose and meaning of any biblical passage under discussion.[12] But it is the realities themselves with which the Bible is basically concerned—birth and life, sin and salvation, time and eternity—whatever may be the

[11] For a modern presentation of this case, see John W. Wenham, *Christ and the Bible*, Tyndale Press 1972.

[12] It must not be concluded that a conservative view of the Bible, which this section involves, requires the rejection of critical scholarship and its methods. See, for example, G. E. Ladd, *The New Testament and Criticism*, Hodder and Stoughton 1970; and Michael Green in *Evangelicals Today*, John C. King (ed.), Hodder and Stoughton 1973, Ch. 3, 'Evangelicals, Honesty and New Testament Study', pp. 31–44.

cultural setting. And all of these realities are seen as before the changeless God, another factor producing a vital link between first and twentieth centuries. The degree of interpretation and application required may grow as time goes on—but the realities do not change. It is about these that the Bible really speaks—and remains normative for us today.

Lastly, as already hinted in a different form, all the other presuppositions of worship have their source material in the Bible. God, Jesus, the Holy Spirit, man, church, world, all are extensively described and interpreted in the pages of the Bible. Our worship is greatly enriched when we learn to relate to the Bible, understand its original meanings and discover its current applications. And this is not the task for scholars alone, but for all the people of God. Worship will be one place in which together we can make discoveries in this direction.

Chapter Seven

WITH THE SACRAMENTS

FEW ASPECTS of religious life are more normally associated with Christianity than the Sacraments of Baptism and Holy Communion. Two focal points of many church interiors are the table/altar and the font/baptistry. Yet few features more typically represent our divisions within Christendom. There are Christian groups who do not practise the sacramental life in this way; the Salvation Army and the Society of Friends, for example. Then there are varieties of belief and administration amongst those who do; differences between denominations and differences of high, low and middle churchmanship within denominations. In this way the sacramental actions which signify entry into the one Church and growth within its life have become a rallying point for its division.

This is all so very sharply contrasted with the emphasis in the New Testament, where the 'one Baptism' and the 'one Bread' are intended to be grounds of Christian unity. Yet we must ask ourselves realistically why such emphases needed to be made in the New Testament. The answer is that, sadly, the signs of division appeared very early in the life of the young church. Racism, morals, spiritual pride, partisanship and sectarianism, false doctrine and apostasy all threatened to split the new communities of Christians. Against these, as a rallying point for unity, New Testament writers pointed among other things to Baptism and the Lord's Supper (I Cor. 12 and Eph. 4 are two obvious examples).

The main point of significance for our study, however, is that the writers draw attention not so much to the fact of the sacraments as to their meaning. It was the understanding of what Baptism and the Lord's Supper represented which was meant effectively to unite the early believers. Emphasis upon simply joining together in these acts plainly did not do so. We are therefore obliged—in harmony with the rest of this book—

to enquire about the basic meaning of our sacramental life; to do so against a background of diverse points of view; and yet to do so in the belief that proper insight into basic sacramental realities will exert a unifying influence upon us.

We begin with the 'God-orientation' of the sacraments. Both Baptism and the Lord's Supper derive their point from the purpose and activity of God. They depend for their meaning upon God's activity in Christ to make new life available to mankind. Both affirm that this activity found its climax in the death and resurrection of Christ. Sacramental action therefore begins by stressing the priority of God's offer over our response; of God's love over our deserving; of the provision of salvation over our claiming of it or entering into it. In this sense (quite apart from the debate about 'what actually happens' in sacramental worship), the basic movement on which the sacraments rely is the movement from God to man,[1] that movement in which God's love reached out through grace and offered new life in Jesus Christ.[2]

To this extent a sacrament will always reflect the unequal balance between the two factors involved—God's grace and our response.[3] No matter how a denomination or local congregation define the 'qualification' for participation in sacramental worship—in terms of training, initiation or experience—there will always be an overwhelming imbalance in favour of the sheer, breathtaking affirmation that God the creator has acted in love towards His creatures so that salvation

[1] For the significance and use of the concept of time where God's saving acts are concerned, and especially their efficacy in past, present and future (a very relevant part of sacramental thought), see A. Weiser, *The Psalms*, S.C.M. (Old Testament Library) 1962, p. 44.

[2] John Reumann gives a fascinating twist to this theme by approaching the idea of worship, not through the English word with its Anglo-Saxon origin in 'worship', but through the German *Gottesdienst* 'service of God', which in German Evangelical tradition is taken as 'God serving us'; 'God doing something for us which we cannot do for ourselves'. Thus the basis of worship is God's saving activity, 'word and sacraments are God's service to the community', to which the church responds by service of God in the world. See Ferdinand Hahn, op. cit., Editor's Introduction, p. xvi–xvii. However one feels about this approach as a total interpretation of worship, it accords well with this particular aspect of sacramental thought.

[3] For consideration of the way in which various sacramental traditions relate these two elements in the matter of Baptism, see *Epworth Review*, Vol. I, No. 1, January 1974, 'Baptism and Membership in the Methodist Church in relation to the current Ecumenical Debate', pp. 6of, by Donald English.

is available. Whether it be passing 'under' the water, or eating bread and drinking wine, the message is plain. Christ's dying and rising are the foundation of all sacramental life.

It is at this point that the 'memorialists'—that is, those who view the Lord's Supper[4] as only a memorial of His death—are at their strongest. They do not wish to emphasize what is 'happening' now at the sacrament except in relation to the remembering, lest they should diminish the historical basis in the events of Christ's earthly ministry. What may or may not be happening now, or what we feel to be happening now, can never become the basis of our salvation. The stress on memorial underscores the fact that sacramental faith has a firm historical basis (a view which is not, of course, limited to memorialists).

This may prove an encouragement to those who are diffident about sacramental worship because they feel themselves to be unworthy to participate, or because when they do take part in it they 'feel' nothing. They contrast themselves with those who both long to come to the sacrament and who seem to feel immensely satisfied by it. The encouragement now offered to any such is two-fold. On the one side unworthiness is not a disqualification—it comes nearer to being a qualification, since the basis of the sacraments is the death and resurrection of Jesus Christ for sinners. It is those who feel themselves to be worthy to partake, or who never give a thought to the possibility of unworthiness, who give more grounds for concern. On the other side there is an encouragement from the fact that the appeal to history is not in the first place directed to our emotions anyway. It does not ask, 'Do you feel that such-and-such is happening?' but 'Do you believe that such-and-such happened?' Its first approach is to knowledge and faith. I will not feel worthy, and I may not feel moved, but I can know that (if not altogether how) the death and resurrection of Jesus Christ provides the basis of my participation in sacramental worship and in that conviction I am encouraged to come.

It is sad that such an approach has been obscured from two different directions by some Christians whose main concern in

[4] Outlines of the major questions and projected answers in connection with the Lord's Supper are to be found in E. L. Mascall, 'Eucharist, Eucharistic Theology', article in Alan Richardson (ed.), *A Dictionary of Christian Theology*, S.C.M. 1969, pp. 116ff., and Ronald S. Wallace, 'Communion, Holy', in J. D. Douglas (ed.), *The New International Dictionary of the Christian Church*, Paternoster 1974, pp. 244ff.

this matter would be to commend the sacramental life. Those for whom sacramental worship is deeply satisfying *emotionally* can so easily and unwittingly weaken the christian tradition of reliance upon historical foundations by testimony to their own rich experience in the sacraments. For those to whom such heights are not (yet—or ever?) within reach, such testimony can move the centre of attraction away from God's acts in history to their feelings in the sacrament; from cause to effect. What is more it focuses attention upon an effect which is also dependent upon such variable factors as personality, state of health and environmental conditioning. This is in no sense intended to decry that proper emotional satisfaction which many of us derive from participation in sacramental worship, nor to seek to inhibit testimony to or discussion of it. It is rather to seek to establish the fact that it cannot be the prime foundation of sacramental life and that too much emphasis upon it may well hinder others for whom it is not or can not be the same. We must concentrate our gaze upon prime causes rather than secondary effects if we are to find the unity we need at this point.

This leads to the second way in which the importance of historical foundations of the sacraments may be unintentionally undermined, namely in the debate about the effectuality of a sacrament. It is unlikely that anyone would wish to deny the importance of this issue—brought very much to the fore at and since the Reformation—since it raises the question of what God is doing now within the life of the Church, and particularly in its worship. Nevertheless this too must be seen as a dependent feature of the sacramental life rather than as an originative one. Without God's activity in Christ neither Christian sacrament would be meaningful or even intelligible. The loss of historical rootage removes the effective point of symbolism, even though the Christ events themselves point to deeper realities in the very nature of God Himself. Discussion about the effectuality of a sacrament can only properly take place when one is clear about that in relation to which the concept of effectuality begins to be meaningful, namely God's saving acts in Christ.

Our sacramental Christian life takes place against an historical background which constantly recalls us to our 'first love', continually reminds us that our dependence is upon that which originated outside us and before us, incessantly points us away from ourselves to God, and invites us first 'to remember'. We shall never be able to dispose with the past tense in our sacramental services.

Yet we must at once move on to a second element in our consideration. We cannot deal only in the past tense. Here the memorialist position is in danger of over-balancing us in the other direction. Certainly God's saving acts are prior; God's grace is always prevenient. Yet God is not locked up in history, limited to past activity. What is more we are invited to enter into the meaning and benefit of His saving activity now. God not only *was* active in Jesus Christ; He is still active today. This involves a present relationship, in which response from us plays a part. The story of Pentecost, as Luke tells it in Acts, reveals that some hearers of Peter's preaching grasped this. 'What are we to do?' they asked. 'Repent and be baptized', Peter replied (Acts 2:37–38). As God's grace elicits a response of faith from us a conscious, willing relationship is established; a relationship which can be called 'saving', because within it we discover our true purpose before God, and the enabling to fulfil it. In the context of this purposeful God-given relationship the sacraments find their place, for they both express and develop the basis and experience of this kind of life. For this reason there must be adequate emphasis upon what is *now* happening in a sacrament. We cannot merely look back, or we shall be ignoring God's presence in our lives today. The fact and nature of our encounter with the Risen Lord must be given proper place.

It is evident that the early Christians were well aware of this point too, though not in the limited field of the sacraments only, but across the whole range of Christian experience. Indeed it is fair to say that we come at this stage to the normative principle of the Christian life day by day, and that the sacramental is one route by which we arrive at a clearer understanding of it, and along which we give expression to it. In passing we may observe that the failure of Christians to distinguish between the basic principle and its various forms of expression has been one of the most fruitful sources of division within Christendom. Perhaps it is because the principle itself is so wide-ranging in its implications that we find it easier to cut it down by channelling it into one area of understanding only. But we must first look at the principle and then observe how it relates to its different forms of expression, including the sacramental.

It can be stated with great simplicity, though in a variety of metaphor. Jesus is recorded as speaking of 'hating' everyone and everything that is dear to us, for His sake; of 'taking up the cross', of 'renouncing' all that we have. These are said to be the basic requirements of a disciple (Luke 14:25–33). Paul writes about being 'crucified with Christ' (Gal. 2.20). The corollary in the case of Jesus is to 'follow' Him, and in the case of Paul to be 'risen with Christ'. Here we are at the heart of Christian living. The faith response by which one becomes a Christian is seen to be more than an intellectual assent to certain truths, more than a grateful affirmation of something done on one's behalf; more even than a receiving of the offer of new life. It is nothing less than the placing of one's life into someone else's hands, risking all in a single new relationship which is to take precedence over everything else, recharting the course of one's life on the basis of a single new 'reading'.[5] It is more even than that, however. We could do all the above (and perhaps some do), and still stand apart from the major events of Christ's ministry in the message of the early church—His death and resurrection. But we are not invited to offer our lives to Him *because of* His dying and rising. We are asked to *enter with Him into* His dying and rising. New Testament writers make it abundantly clear that we do not in this way add to Christ's atoning work. That was 'once for all' and complete long before we even existed. But faith relationship to Christ means going the way of death to self and risen life to God as a daily experience, the normative factor, the governing principle of one's life.

It is precisely here that we see another side of the priority of God's grace. He not only makes the prior offer: He also establishes the nature of the relationship within which the offer may be taken up. And He does so by the manner of His self-giving. In Jesus Christ we see the embodiment of total, unrestricted self-giving. Dying and rising are the working out in time and space of this basic principle of the universe. The offer

[5] For an outline of the various ways in which faith is understood in the New Testament, see Donald English, 'Faith in the New Testament', in John Stacey (ed.), *About Faith*, Epworth 1972 pp. 28ff.

of salvation is the offer to join one's life to that fundamental principle. This is why Jesus speaks of putting Him before all else as the *beginning* of the way of discipleship; not because at the outset we achieve this, but because from the outset those are the terms of the relationship, terms which take a life-time and beyond to realize and explore. But we begin at this level of quality (not quantity). Now we can see the seriousness of the life/death contrasts in the teaching of Jesus and Paul. This is why the man who seeks to save his life will lose it, but the man who loses His life for Christ and the Kingdom will gain it for ever (Matt. 10:39; Mark 8:35; Luke 17:33; John 12:25). This is why Paul can protest 'I die everyday' (I Cor. 15:31). It was neither joke nor exaggeration; it was the statement of the basic principle of true Christian living.

It is at this point that the process of 'narrowing by selection' has taken place within Christian thought. Some have applied this principle exclusively to the inner life of the believer, in the battle against evil within and the search for personal holiness. Others have looked wholly outward to positive action for the Kingdom in everyday life. Each has tended to scorn the other, and yet each in his own way has sought to take dying and rising seriously. Still others have interpreted this principle in sacramental terms. As we turn to do so now we make a strong plea that all three ways need one another for the fullest expression of the basic principle to which each relates.

The sacraments do so relate. Our services of baptism, whether the carrying of a helpless child or the immersion of a willing adult, each symbolize the placing of a life beneath the water. In this way the total nature of the Christian commitment is portrayed. At the Lord's Table the act of eating bread and drinking wine in the context of the story of the Last Supper and the account of the crucifixion; then the offering of ourselves as living sacrifices,[6] underlines the same theme. The prime point of reference is the once-for-all death of Christ with the subsequent resurrection. Next is our faith relationship to God in Christ, a relationship of daily dying and rising. And now in the sacrament both the historical fact and the existential relationship are joined and affirmed. Moreover the relationship is deepened, since the givenness of God thus symbolized never decreases:

[6] See Ch. 4 for the implications of this allusion in Romans 12.

5

and since we on our part are renewing our living sacrifice in actions and words. As with the rest of our Christian life, the sacraments are 'from faith to faith'.

It is in this setting that the presence of Christ in the sacraments should be considered, not primarily in relation to the state of certain material objects or the special significance of particular moments, or even the importance of specific words or sentences. It is within the ethos of the faith relationship, built as it is upon response to God's grace in Christ, that the sacraments must be understood as the vehicle of Christ's presence. It is as the Holy Spirit works within that relationship, deepening it as the significance of the symbols enriches our understanding of and response to the gospel, that Christ is made known. What matters most is surely that God in Christ by the Holy Spirit is giving Himself yet again, as He did supremely in Christ once in history in a never-to-be-repeated way, and that in the sharing of symbols, actions and words which vividly bring meaning to such giving we renew our faith response and self-giving. Within that relationship Christ is present and known.

Have we any grounds for affirming that Christ is 'specially' present in the sacraments? In terms of a deepening faith relationship it is difficult to assert this. 'And be assured, I am with you always, to the end of time', are the words recorded of Him (Matt. 28:20). He is surely not more or less present on differing occasions. One great basis of sacramental thinking is the constant availability of Christ's presence. Yet we may surely say that Christ is 'uniquely' present in the sacraments, and that for two reasons. First, certain material objects are used and explanatory words associated in these services only. Moreover, these material objects and particular words are used precisely because in the Christian tradition Jesus is recorded as having commanded them so to be used. Thus the uniqueness stems, not from the *degree* or *specialness* of His presence, but from the origin of this way in which His people know His presence, an origin rooted in words of His, in actions of His, and in the experience of the early Christians when the Risen Christ appeared at meals with them. In this sense 'unique' does not mean better than, but different from. The important thing for us is that, wherever else He is present, He *is* present in our sacramental services.

There is, however, another dimension as far as the present significance of the sacraments is concerned. It is different from our personal relationship with Christ, but not detached from it. This is our relationship with other Christians. In neither Baptism nor Eucharist can one properly be 'alone with Christ'. Both are essentially corporate acts. In both, the 'I' and 'they' are obliterated by the 'we' and 'us'. There is one baptism (in whatever form), one loaf (however presented and taken) and one cup (however shaped and offered). And there is one body of Christ on earth—God's people in Christ, by His choice. Hence Paul's horror at Corinthian Christians dividing over partisanship, greed or gifts. Hence, too, the stern warning by the writer to the Hebrews about those who, having entered into the household of God through the veil of Christ's flesh, and the shedding of His blood, and having been inwardly and outwardly cleansed, now 'stay away from our meetings' (Heb. 10:19–25 N.E.B.). We are inevitably one, because in Christ all are one. And in Baptism and the Lord's Supper we receive again, affirm again and share again, the essential oneness which Christ gives. Not only is the presence of Christ a reality in the sacraments: the presence of my brethren is also important and significant.

So far we have argued that the sacramental life must gain its first perspective by a backward look which recalls its historical foundations in God's grace revealed in Christ in a once-for-all way. Next we have affirmed that in the present the sacraments are to be understood in terms of our faith relationship to Christ, based on the principle of dying and rising with Him, and that within that relationship the presence of Christ and the presence of our brethren are deeply meaningful. But one more dimension remains, summed up in the words, 'until He comes'.

'For every time you eat this bread and drink this cup, you proclaim the death of the Lord, until He comes.' So wrote Paul to the Corinthians (I Cor. 11:26). Certainly the Christian, from his vantage point in the present, reflects upon the significance of the historical events of Christ. But this is not the only direction of his gaze. There is another pole to the Christian's world. Salvation is not only historical and existential; it is also eschatological—it is concerned with the end time. Jesus is recorded as speaking of the Kingdom of God.[7] Its inception is probably to be dated from His earthly ministry; its establishment brought much further on in His death and resurrection; and its growth continued as God the Holy Spirit has added to the Church in every age since.[8] But the final consummation is still regarded as being in the future.[9] Since the Kingdom was introduced by Christ the Christian now knows that he lives in the end time. But he also perceives the partial nature of the kingdom thus far. He sees past events in Christ as the pledge of things to come, when the completion of God's plan of love will be seen, and God will be 'all in all'. Thus faith and hope are joined in the daily experience of the Christian.

Of this healthy tension between past and future, experienced in the present, our sacraments speak. Baptism depends for its meaning upon the saving events in Christ: but it also introduces us into the community who live in hope, the pilgrim people of God, daily making their way towards the final consummation of God's Kingdom. In the Lord's Supper, too, we are made dramatically aware of the past events which are so basic. Yet we also remind ourselves that we are showing forth His death until He comes. In the tension between past activity of God, accessible to faith; and the future fulfilment, looked for in hope; we are enriched and encouraged in the present by the presence of Christ in the context of the church through the sacraments.

Later (ch. 9) we shall look more fully into the three-dimensional nature of the Christian outlook on life. Here we pause only to plead that our view of the sacraments, in their essential meaning, should be guided by such a concept, and that we search for their meaning, and for our unity around that as we affirm their dependence upon God's initiative in the saving events of Christ; as we discover Christ's presence within the faith relationship of dying and rising (and in so doing

[7] There are references in all the Gospels, though they are not nearly so numerous in John.

[8] For an outline of this approach to the establishing of the kingdom, see J. R. W. Stott, *Men with a Message*, Longmans 1954, Ch. 1, 'The Message of Jesus'. For articles see 'Kingdom of God' in the New International Dictionary, op. cit., and the bibliographies in each.

[9] One makes this statement while aware of the great debate over the nature and content of the Christian's hope for the future. Yet in so far as all Christians do have hope the sentence can stand.

become more intensely aware of the presence of our brethren, too); and as we learn to live in hope that all that we celebrate in the sacraments is moving forward in the purposes of God towards a final consummation. In these eternal realities, and in our responses of faith, love and hope, is there not enough both to satisfy and to unite us in our sacramental worship?

Chapter Eight

IN THE WORLD

TO MY MIND one of the most alarming types of opening prayer in worship is that which begins with words like, 'O Lord, we thank you that we are able to come away from the rush and bustle of everyday life and withdraw into your presence here in your house.' I think I know what such a prayer is seeking to say, and I can believe that the harassed housewife and mother, or the worried business executive, or the exhausted manual worker, find comfort in it. But the implications about the character and concerns of the worship thus introduced, and even about the character and concerns of the God thus worshipped, are somewhat alarming. For such prayers speak of a desire to forget that one belongs to the world, and for a brief time to play at not belonging. What is more, the game of 'not belonging' is played in the presence of a God who seems, by the definitions of the game, not to belong either. If we meet Him here when we come away from the busy world, presumably we leave Him again when we go back to it?

If it were only a matter of the opening prayer, on some occasions, giving such an impression, one would have little cause, or less cause, for concern. But it is so easy for the whole of our worship to be offered in the atmosphere of 'withdrawal' from an alien world that we almost produce a two-compartmentalized outlook on life amongst the worshippers.

This is undoubtedly why, in the past few years, there has been increasing debate about whether our priorities in Christian thinking should be represented by the formula 'God-World-Church', or by what is said to be the false, traditional pattern, 'God-Church-World'.[1] This is not the place to enter into that

---

[1] See, for example, J. G. Davies, *Worship and Mission*, S.C.M. 1966, J. G. Davies, *Dialogue with the World*, S.C.M. 1967, and J. C. Hoekendijk, *The Church Inside Out*, S.C.M. 1967. It was put to the World Council of Churches at Evanston by D. T. Niles in the following words, 'God's conversation with his church is a conversation about the world. The church must be prepared to speak about the world if it wants to speak with God. The world is the direct object of God's activity.'

debate, which is, in any case, plentifully written about and well documented. But that controversy does remind us of the fact that no worshipper can gainsay, or ought to forget, namely that all our worship is offered within the context of life in the world, and that it must be properly related to it or we shall find ourselves living divided lives and so declaring the larger part of our existence to be outside the control or domain of God.

Before exploring the implications of such a statement, and looking for a Christian clue to the solution of the problem, it is probably worth while to pause for one moment to be clear about definitions where the word 'world' is concerned. The varying connotations which it can bear will already have determined some 'reader reaction' to what has gone before in this chapter. The biblical use of the word and the concept provides a good guide for us here. The 'world' is spoken of as that which God created and which He loves (John 3:16, for example). But, conversely, it is also used of mankind 'over against' God; man in rebellion against God and displaying characteristics which typify godlessness (I John 2:15–17, for example). These the New Testament Christians were told to avoid. Since each is a description of the same geographical and human area it is hardly surprising that the two have vied for supremacy in the thought of Christians, and that much confusion has ensued. By 'world' in this chapter we mean that which God made and loves, but within which man's open rebellion takes place. We are therefore combining the two New Testament uses and seeking to face the fact that both characteristics are present in the life of society around us, that our worship must enable us to be aware of that fact, and that it should also assist us to distinguish between the two elements so as to have a proper relationship to each.

Why is it that the Church seems to be such an easy target for criticism about lack of awareness of the world outside its doors? There are at least two answers to this question. The first concerns *the Church's view of herself*. Our definition of what it means to be the Church vitally affects our awareness of the world. The second concerns *the Church's understanding of the world*. What we know about the world, and how we understand what we know will largely determine our awareness of the relationship of the Church to society round about (and will also, incidentally, do a great deal to influence the shape of the life of the local church). We look at each of these in turn.

First our definition of the Church. Bishop Stephen Neill outlines this point very clearly in his book *The Church and Christian Union* (Oxford 1968). He quotes four traditional definitions of the Church: the Augsburg Confession of 1530 (Lutheran), Article XIX of the Thirty-Nine Articles (Anglican) the Heidelberg Catechism of 1563 (Reformed), and a statement by Robert Cardinal Bellarmine in 1590 (Roman Catholic) (pp. 73–4). On the basis of these he concludes, 'One thing stands out plainly from each of these four definitions, as from many similar statements which might be cited—all are set forth in terms of being and not of function' (p. 75). A little later he asserts, 'At this point it is borne in upon us that no satisfactory definition of the Church can be arrived at in terms only of its own existence. We have to ask not merely "What is the Church?", but also, "What is the Church for?" ' (p. 75). He pleads for the substitution of a dynamic for a static ecclesiology. He offers as a definition along these lines the following: 'The Church is that body of men through which it is the will of God that the Gospel of everlasting salvation through Christ should be proclaimed to all men everywhere, to the ends of the earth and to the end of time' (p. 76).

We need not stay to discuss that particular definition. Its value lies in the attention it pays to the concept that the Church has a responsibility in the world and to the world. Bishop Neill refers to it as 'the missionary dimension'. Without this sense of defining the Church in relation to its world setting we will constantly end up with static definitions which stultify our worship.

For example, if we have no sense of having to relate to the daily life of society around us our worship can easily be seen as being solely for our own benefit. Witness the traditional Methodist way of enquiring about the morning's worship: 'Did you have a good time today?' (To which the reply will usually be, 'Yes, *he* was very good this morning', or, 'No, I couldn't follow *him*'.) '*He*' is not, as you might be pardoned for thinking, the Almighty, but the preacher thus elevated to the point of deity or reduced to the level of ecclesiastical entertainer. At a deeper level still, and therefore a more serious one, there is the tendency to assess worship by the degree of interest or personal benefit gained from it. Of course one would hope that worship would be for us all enjoyable, interesting and beneficial, but when these become not only important criteria but the exclusive criteria we are in a very dangerous state, for God has now become nothing more than a help to our spiritual growth, or even our religious entertainment.

A second dangerous by-product of worship which lacks a sense of world setting is a deterioration in the attitude and participation of the worshippers. Since worship is largely for the in-group there often develops a lack of urgency about it, a failure to take part in something which is absolutely vital, wholly necessary to daily living; something upon which the rest of the week depends for its meaningfulness. Rather it becomes something we have chosen to do, much as others will at the same time be choosing to play golf or to go to the public house. The whole atmosphere loses its sense of electrifying urgency.

Allied to this is the triviality of much of the subject matter as a result. Since it is for our sake we can afford to reduce the material to manageable proportions. Having forgotten the world outside we have now absolved ourselves from facing the great issues of living in the modern world; the problems of suffering, injustice, pollution, starvation; the question of meaning, of liberation, even of salvation. We are now under no real pressure to bother with them if our moments of worship are meant to be a haven from the pressures of the 'world outside'. And much of the triviality of our worship—both in its selfishness and its lack of challenge—comes from just this source.

It is not a long step from this point to the next, to a false security which passes for some form of Christian assurance. Since the actual content of the worship has been progressively debased by a lack of urgency, challenge and large themes, many worshippers are at a loss to find any spiritual security in the content itself. Almost imperceptibly, therefore, the ground of their assurance ceases to be the content of the worship and becomes more easily identifiable with the actual form of the service; the order in which events take place; and even the very phraseology of the services. It is difficult otherwise to explain the degree of opposition often met from the congregation if the order of worship is changed. The amount of heat generated is often out of all proportion to the extent of the change suggested. But it is perfectly explicable if the very order of service, the very sequence of events, and even the language itself has now become the actual raft of safety for the worshipper. (Again one must add a point of explanation. It is obvious that the order of a service does contribute something to the meaning of the service, as does the language used. They can indeed point to the very nature of the gospel. This is not in dispute here. What is not healthy, however, is a reliance upon a form of service or of words whose meaning has ceased to matter, since the actual progression through them has become the only thing that really counts.)

Perhaps the most terrifying possibility of all that emerges from the static view of the Church is the attitude towards the person conducting worship. He or she so easily becomes the servant of the congregation, there to lead them at their level, to help them in their situation, to please them in their worship. The cosy atmosphere of the worshipping community is not to be disturbed by the large questions of everyday life. The prophetic voice becomes unwelcome and embarrassing. The ecclesiastical mechanic may certainly tell us how well the engine runs, and even help us to hear it doing so as we sit in the car with him. But he must not attempt to drive the car out through the garage doors into the alien world, for out there are other cars, driven on different principles from ours, and threatening the well-being of our car. Mileage on the clock is a dangerous aim, to be discouraged. In any case, one can hear the engine better in the quietness of the garage, and without any competition from other cars.

All of this is challenged (and the picture above is, of course, overdrawn for effect), by the 'missionary dimension', or simply by the sense that there is a world in which we have to live the Christian life we celebrate in worship, in which we have to serve the God whom here we worship, in which all our presuppositions will be challenged, and where men and women need what here we enjoy. With such awareness we feel we must ask the big questions, must worship the God whose world it is, must try to discern the nature of His presence in that world and the form of His mission in it that we may join Him there. We feel that there is no time for responding to our own petty foibles, or having everything which pleases us. We must worship with the awareness of the world pressing in upon us, for the God we worship was there as we came to worship and will be there when we go out. All this brings us to the second factor in this awareness; our understanding of the world.

It is easy to understand why Christians are accused of not understanding the world around them, for in this we are very little different from anyone else. Can any modern man claim to understand his world? The rate of change is so staggering that by the time one comes to see a thing clearly it has altered its form. If one speaks in general terms then one is immediately reminded that the situation varies from place to place and moment to moment. And modern life is made up of such a complex of inter-locking forces that one would need to be an expert in any number of fields to begin to make sense of it. (This is simply illustrated by asking such questions as 'Why was Mr A declared redundant at fifty?', or 'Why did Mrs B's marriage break up?' or 'Why is our national economy in such a parlous state?'. The number of contributory factors in any of the answers to such questions might understandably daunt the amateur.) No wonder many of us don't bother, and that our worship as a result virtually ignores the problems except in a general committing of everything into God's hands.

Yet there are two points at which we must make the effort to understand the world around us. One concerns the *general characteristics of the culture* (or myriad of sub-cultures) in which we live and offer our worship. The other is the specific points at which *that culture actually changes the shape of the Church* itself, and may do so unhelpfully if we are not aware that it is doing so. (One striking example is the emergence since the last war of Sunday morning service as the main one of the day. Did that depend upon church decisions based upon theological and pastoral considerations: or did it result from the influence of television, the family car, the social pressure to visit grandparents, and the pattern of work life which has evolved?) In both cases—general features and specific points of contact—we can only be selective in the hope of deepening the awareness in worshippers which will reveal much more than can be listed here.

We begin with general features. First is the *anthropocentric* nature of our culture—its over-riding concern about man himself. Before rushing to criticize such a position we should note how much good derives from it. When man decides to neglect the divine in his thinking, and to concentrate on the human, the practical outcome often looks promising. For example, he cannot any longer leave any problem to God! The result is that he bends his energies to doing what he can. In so doing he often shames Christians who are tempted to leave too many things to God when they could be God's servants in putting them right. No assessment of our culture could be accurate if it ignored the vast amount of good-will exhibited when need of certain kinds is made known. (While this chapter was being written there was a newspaper report of an appeal for money to buy a kidney machine for a little girl in a certain town. Before the organizers could get the appeal properly launched the money had all come in, from all kinds of sources —some very moving—and a request had to be made that no more be contributed.) A man-centred culture gets some things done with astonishing speed and efficiency, particularly at the practical level.[2]

Yet it is not all gain, and particularly at the deeper level of principles of living. We may take as illustration three of the major philosophical systems which in their non-Christian form challenge Christianity in our culture. The first is Communism. Its concern for a just world in which each man plays his proper role in the interests of the whole group is well known, and in some places extremely effective. One visitor to China recently commented that they had even 'legislated sin away'. The method is tellingly described by some words of Lenin: 'With this machine, or rather this weapon [the state], we shall crush every form of exploitation, and when there are no longer any possibilities of exploitation left on earth, no more people owning land or factories, no more people gorging themselves under the eyes of others who are starving, when such things are impossible, then and only then shall we cast this machine aside. . . . And

---

[2] See, as an example, Soviet Russia and Communist China. See also Horst Symonowski's contrast between villagers in India crying to their gods for rain, and others who worked at a cement factory and had no such sense of dependence. *The Christian Witness in an Industrial Society*, Collins 1966, pp. 48–9.

when, on an earth which has finally been subdued and purged
of enemies, the final iniquity shall have been drowned in the
blood of the just and the unjust, then the State ... will be
discreetly absorbed into the silent city of Justice.'[3] The very
moving vision, and the deeply serious intent of that passage
underline the enormous potential of a man-centred approach
to living. And many who would not call themselves communist
would probably subscribe in general terms to a philosophy of
politics which was not far removed from the main lines of
Lenin's thinking.

The same would be true of Humanism. If slightly less
rigorous and dour, the humanist philosophy offers a similar
invitation to build a better world. In the words of Dr Corliss
Lamont, 'Naturalistic Humanism challenges men to rely on
their own intelligence, courage and effort in building their
happiness and fashioning their destiny in a world of infinite
possibilities.'[4] Or, as H. J. Blackham put it, 'The humanist
aspires to use past, present and future, life and death, the arts
and sciences, ideas and ideals, along with all other resources as
developing means of achieving the better possibilities open to
him.'[5] Even more than Communism, such a philosophy of
human self-help towards a great new future has enormous
appeal, even to many who could not define Humanism yet
nevertheless would subscribe to its basic tenets. (And we might
ask, in passing, whether much of what we say and hear in
worship is not thinly disguised Humanism, with a 'God-bit'
thrown in for tradition's sake.)

More complex and almost haunting in its influence is
Existentialism. Its awareness of the shallowness of most human
life compared with the depths really present is well brought out
by words of Colin Wilson in *The Outsider*. 'The Outsider's case
against society is very clear. All men and women have ...
dangerous, unnamable impulses, yet they keep up a pretence,
to themselves, to others; their respectability, their philosophy,
their religion, are all attempts to gloss over, to make look
civilized and rational something that is savage, unorganized,

---

[3] Lecture at the Sverdlov University, quoted in Albert Camus, *The Rebel*,
Penguin 1962; pp. 198–9.
[4] Quoted in H. J. Blackham (ed.), *Objections to Humanism*, Penguin 1965, p. 23.
[5] Ibid., p. 122.

irrational. He is an Outsider because he stands for Truth.'[6]
But how does one respond when faced with such depths of
personality in a world which constantly asks us to decide when
we never seem to have sufficient data for proper decision-
making processes? Sartre's hero, Roquentin (if hero is the right
word) sums up one characteristic existentialist response in the
book *Nausea*. 'I was just thinking,' he says at the meal table
'. . . that here we are, all of us, eating and drinking to preserve
our precious existence, and there's nothing, nothing, absolutely
no reason for existing.'[7] How many people around us who may
never have heard of existentialism, nevertheless live on the
basis of 'what-the-hellism'? The appeal, in a world so complex
and confusing, of a way of thinking which denies all ultimate
meaning anyway, or at least denies that it could be available
to us, is very great, and many live on just such a basis for all
practical purposes.

Of course to say that such philosophies are attractive does not
mean that they are either successful or desirable. For all
Communism's high ideals, for example, we know that treatment
of thinkers like Solzhenitzyn, or of the underground church,
reveals the inability of the system to give proper scope to the
individual. Humanism, on its own admission, has not yet
found that which satisfies the sense of awe which men feel.
Atheistic Existentialism is not able to live by its own attitude
to meaning, as Sartre himself has shown in his own life. And all
three fail to come to terms with what for Christians is the
'God-dimension' of life, which for us is so basic.

Such a brief reference to large topics does not, of course, do
them justice. But it does serve a useful purpose nevertheless.
It does so by raising the question, 'Do these great themes which
are so evidently pressing upon men and women today (or these
movements would have no followers), really find a place in our
worship? Are our prayers, our hymns, our sermons, our
meditations facing up to questions about meaning, justice,
individuality and mutual concern, responsibility to fashion a
better world, the despair felt by so many of our fellows?' To
put it at its simplest, 'Could a stranger to our culture guess its
major concerns and problems by attending our worship?'

[6] Colin Wilson, *The Outsider*, Pan Books 1963, p. 12.
[7] Jean-Paul Sartre, *Nausea*, Penguin 1965, p. 162.

If the God we worship is the 'Sovereign Lord of heaven and earth and sea and everything in them' (Acts 4:24), then it ought surely to be so. Even more, 'Would he discern in our worship that we have something distinctive to contribute in such areas because our worship has included them?' The Christian Church seems to have found it easier to concern itself *either* with answers from a living God *or* with questions from a living world. Our worship needs to be experienced at the meeting points between the two, without avoiding the implications of either. The divisions within Christendom caused by opting for one or the other also prevent other men and women from hearing both the question put and the answer discerned, which is another way of saying that our evangelism is less effective than it might be because we have not ourselves guarded the whole message and its application.

Our culture has another major characteristic which should cause deep thought as we contemplate our worship. It is a *scientific* culture. One need hardly elucidate that point, but its significance is worth pondering. The scientific revolution ushered in the technological age. The technological age makes the practical solution of many of life's problems only a matter of time. The solving of problems of living technologically means that man plays a much greater part in making his environment what he wants it to be. Part of what he wants it to be is comfortable, desirable and enjoyable. The more this life is enjoyed the less does talk about life hereafter seem of pressing importance. One can, of course, point to pollution, personal unhappiness, large-scale methods of killing, man's inhumanity to man and many other facets of modern life to show how limited the improvements are. But this does not alter the basic fact that life for the majority in our culture is much less burdensome than it was for our grandparents. There is a much greater degree of variety, opportunity and availability where the 'good things of life are concerned'. In such areas there may be less inclination to consider questions raised by religion.

Another result of the scientific revolution is a rejection by many of the idea of the supernatural. Even when the limitations of scientific method are admitted it remains true that science has advanced because of its determination to limit its scope to observable phenomena; to be governed by the empirical and the pragmatic. And since so much has been uncovered, and so much more will yet be uncovered, it is scarcely surprising that claims which cannot be so substantiated, according to scientific method, claims relating to supernatural realms, should be rejected in favour of naturalistic views of life.

All of this leads to a further outcome of the scientific method, a tendency in our society to be suspicious of anything which cannot be known by that method. Can one really speak of 'knowing' anything which has not been scientifically demonstrated, or is not capable of being so demonstrated? One is not here suggesting that leading scientists necessarily view life in this way, but that many men and women with whom we deal have a sneaking suspicion that such is the case, and they live and think accordingly. As Anthony Wesson and Richard Jones put it, science's 'emphasis on experimentation and empirical verification seems diametrically opposed to the Christian talk about faith'.[8]

Such questions take us into the field of Christian apologetics, which is not our concern here. What is our concern, however, is to reflect upon the services of worship we have recently attended, and to ask how much awareness was displayed of the fact that we live in a scientifically based culture. Was there any attempt to relate ideas of the Kingdom of God, or eternal life, to the comfortable technologically serviced life so many of us lead? Was there any exploration of the ideas of the natural and the supernatural? (The question does not pre-judge the answer.) Was there any reflection upon the various ways of 'knowing' which are available to the human mind—each way of knowing appropriate to the material to be known? Again it is much easier simply to ignore the questions raised by our cultural setting or, on the other hand lightly to dismiss previous Christian thought patterns as no longer relevant to the modern age. The plea here is for a proper consideration of both, a consideration which will be natural to worship by Christians aware of the world in which they live and determined in their commitment to the God they worship.

A third main strand in the make-up of our culture setting is what one might call its *freedom fighting*. This is a great age for

[8] R. G. Jones and A. J. Wesson, *Mission and the Death of God*, Methodist Home Mission Occasional Paper 1968, p. 5.

liberation; indeed 'liberation' is probably one of the most overworked words in our vocabulary. And the passion to set free takes a number of forms. There is its anti-authoritarian shape. All forms of artificial authority are under attack today. If anyone holds an office which in the past would of itself command respect, then today he must earn that respect by his service in that office. 'You must do this because I say so' is one of the simplest formulae for creating resistance, however reasonable one's actual advice might be. A number of armies in the world, surely the last bastion of this kind of authority, have had difficulty in this area of late. Authority has to be earned personally, and can never be assumed.

Another shape of the freedom concern is the anti-moralistic passion of many today. Rules of behaviour, couched in the form of moral behaviour patterns, are extremely suspect. It is the age of 'doing your own thing', of deciding in each new situation what the situation demands or simply what you feel like doing this time. The idea that a set of rules or guide-lines could be adopted as a permanent norm is rejected.

Removal of rules in the sphere of aesthetics is also apparent; in music, art, drama, novels. Thus Colin Crouch wrote in the *Guardian*, 'The emphasis on abstraction, formlessness, *objets trouvés*, and transitoriness is related to the same hostility to all kinds of systemization, the extension to perceptual and cognitive experience of the same perspective of total freedom.' The evident puzzlement of the older generation about what today passes for art, music and literature is a sign of the extent to which the rules have gone. How many sit waiting for the final scene of the television play, the closing section which will draw it all together, only to see the sub-titles which announce that it is in fact over; however inconclusively?

Would our worship communicate to anyone else that we are aware of these great issues? Do we truly experience the liberation of the people of God in our worship; a liberation which both relates to various forms of liberation known in the world, but which at the same time goes beyond anything the world can know of itself? If it is only the former it is not distinctively Christian: if it is only the latter then it is largely irrelevant to what goes on in the world outside. Does our awareness of God's presence in worship; our celebration of the gospel; our

experience of belonging to the Body of Christ and our experience
of the Holy Spirit help us to discern the links between the two—
and the differences?

A fourth, and for us final aspect of our culture is its sense
of *perplexity*. Not only Christian speakers point to this. In his
book *The Faith of the Counsellors*, Paul Halmos describes the lack
of faith in a political solution which has overtaken our fellows.
'The educated man of the west can no longer don the uniform
of a political allegiance without feeling a little ashamed and a
little apologetic about the masquerade, and so he now seems to
prefer to go naked politically.'[9] Even where this is not reflected
in low returns at elections there is a cynicism in much discussion of politics and politicians which is a threat to the proper
working of the democratic system as we know it.

Halmos also points to another element in the perplexity; the
uncertainty about life continuing at all. 'In the twentieth
century medicine has made the premature death of the
individual all but unnecessary, and physics the premature
death of the species almost probable or, at least, almost
certainly possible. We live longer and more healthily, and we
threaten ourselves with extermination. . . . Our extensive
knowledge of the universe is matched only by our vast ignorance
of the proper use to which this knowledge could be put' (p. 11).
These comments are made by him in the role of sociologist.

Yet another expression of the perplexing nature of modern
life relates to the contrast between our vision of freedom and
our setting up of huge business corporations and institutional
structures which so easily dominate our lives in a way which is
almost beyond our awareness, and certainly beyond our
ability to do much about. Professor Galbraith, in his Reith
Lectures, pointed out the fascinating situation in huge American
corporations, where decision-making depends upon the partial
contribution of so many different groups and individuals. When
the material arrives on the desk of the top executive the decision
has in one sense already been dictated by the gathering of the
material. But who actually made that decision? And if it is
wrong how does one unmake it within such a process? And if
these corporations exert such influence upon the lives of their
employees—where they live, where their children are educated,

<hr>

[9] Paul Halmos, *The Faith of the Counsellors*, Constable 1965, p. 15.

how much money they have, and so on, is there not an enormous threat to human freedom there? And this in a culture which is fighting for freedom.

What a contrast such considerations make with the unruffled calm of much of our worship. Of course Christians rightly feel that God is somehow in control of His world, but it would be a more comforting calm if it had emerged from the agonizing awareness of the amount of fear and perplexity current in our society. So often we see Christian 'peace' as the absence of war, inward or outward. But the biblical concept of 'peace' has to do with a positive attitude of mind, a deep-seated trust in God's control even in the midst of the storm. If our worship keeps us from recognizing the storm for what it is, then it also prevents us from entering into the deepest experiences of Christian peace available to us.

So far we have noticed that the view shared by Christians about the definition of the Church will influence her relationship to the world; particularly the presence or absence of a missionary dimension. But we also saw that an understanding of the world, which produced proper awareness, was necessary too. One part of such understanding has to do with the general features of our culture, of which we have noted four. Now we must go on to ask at which points the definition of the Church and the awareness of the world meet. Again we have space to mention only a selection.

First we must surely subject to more careful scrutiny the meaning communicated by many of *the words we use* in our worship. Reference was made earlier to the concept of 'knowing', for example. When we speak or sing or pray about 'knowing God' in our lives, or 'knowing Jesus Christ as our Saviour and Lord'; what exactly is heard and understood by those whose educational background has been controlled by scientific training? If we use the word 'commitment', how aware are we that we speak in a culture which, from the lofty realms of scholarship to the lower slopes of commodity advertising, is constantly taught to commit itself to an idea or a product only so long as it 'does the job', 'delivers the goods', 'gives the best results'? How does this influence the idea of committing oneself to Christ (or to a marriage partner for that matter!), for life? The writer learned in Nigeria how easily an

Igbo word meaning 'eternal life' could be heard by half the
congregation as 'reincarnation'! We need to reflect upon
similar possibilities in our use of familiar words which have (for
us) specific meanings which they do not bear for those
differently educated.

The plea here is not for a glossary of religious terms and their
meaning to be inserted into the back of every service book
(though it might help some), but rather for a greater awareness
of such factors in our worship and a conscious effort on the part
of those who conduct worship and preach to give help to
congregations along this line. Deepening awareness about the
actual meaning of what we do and say in worship, and its
relationship to the world in which we live is surely a priority
for all Christians.

A second point at which the definition of the Church and the
awareness of the world meet is the area of *social concern and
caring*. Here we include such factors as health, social services
and education. How does the life of the Church relate to these?
It is fairly certain that the Church can claim large responsibility
for the beginnings of each of these parts of modern life and of our
welfare state. The question is how we are to relate to them
today. And a very strange answer seems to meet us. Fields
which we at first established are not only now largely occupied
and cared for by others; they are in addition guarded by them
with the result that the representatives of the Church must first
ask permission to enter. The minister requesting permission of
the Ward Sister before embarking upon a visit to a sick member
of his congregation is a clear illustration of this point, and a
'proper' one. So do we fit in, and if so, how and where? Our
answer will be determinative for much of our praying and
thinking in worship.

It is easy here to develop a new 'God of the Gaps' theory. On
this basis the Christian acknowledges that there are many areas
in which he has no contribution to make; areas where the
expertise of the trained professional is required. But, it is argued,
there are points at which we will be necessary—in those gaps
where no one else is trained, able, or even willing to help. For
example, most babies are baptized, most couples married in
church, most burials are religious services of one sort or another.
Less obviously, most social agencies lean heavily upon voluntary

help, of which churches supply a fair amount. And there is always the question of who comforts the ill, or their relatives, and who tells a family that their relative is going to die. The examples are numerous, and the work done in such situations by Christian people is of great importance. But as a theory of Christian involvement in society it is no more satisfactory than was the God of the gaps theory about science, where every gap in man's knowledge was allocated as part of God's residence in the universe, with obvious results.

Without decrying the part played in the gaps, therefore, we need to seek a view which properly reflects the vision of God included in our first chapter. This is most helpfully illustrated and set out in terms of the Hospital by Heije Faber in his book, *Pastoral Care in the Modern Hospital* (S.C.M. 1971). Here he describes the various roles played by the minister in visiting a hospital ward. One of these is simply to be the representative of the Church who in seeking to be this also seeks to represent Christ. In doing this he not only stands alongside other experts, each doing his own job, he also brings a new dimension to the hospital. He 'changes the climate', introduces a new wave-length, a new dimension on the whole of life, the possibility of a relationship with God.

We can helpfully adopt this picture in relation to the whole field we are now considering. Our place is not simply to 'plug the gaps' until welfare state help is provided; honourable though that tradition of Christian service is, and will remain. A much larger task faces us; namely to offer to all social caring the specifically Christian dimension of the whole of life, and to be the presence which embodies it, both through Christians whose professions take them into these areas and also through the voluntary work we undertake. Throughout our task is to embody and interpret the nature of Christ's presence in these sectors of life.

Our worship should reflect such broad concerns. Our awareness of God's presence where sick and needy are cared for; of the struggle for personhood experienced by poor and suffering; of the way in which God's love in Christ is available to all in such a setting; of the challenge to be committed to be channels of such love; and of the need of those Christians in such areas for the loving, sustaining fellowship and prayers of the Church, will all play their part in fashioning the content of worship. Much more important all through is the basic attitude of the worshippers in these matters. What we say and do is almost less important at this point than the attitudes we adopt and the breadth of our concern and understanding, since these will in turn be reflected by deed and action. We need to be delivered from narrow cramping ideas of God's relation to this world of social caring, so that His people may both recognize the extent of His presence and of their privilege in joining Him in ministering to the needy and to those who care for them.

Thirdly, there is the large question of *communications* in the modern world. Are we, as Gavin Reid has argued, moving from a word culture to a picture culture?[10] Does our worship reflect awareness of this or of any other changes in this field? Are we inevitably tied to the exact outline of our present services, tied as it is to certain presuppositions about the way in which people share common convictions and learn from one another? This is not to say that our present ways are of necessity wrong. Such a conclusion does not have to follow, even if our culture does favour other ways of communicating. What does matter is that our changes or our refusal to change should be based on what actually is being learned in the fields of communication and shared experience, and should not arise simply out of a desire for change for its own sake, or conservatism because we do not wish to be disturbed. Greater concern about the best method for communicating that which we wish to communicate and about the best way to share that which we wish to share would be preferable to debates about change or no change as questions in their own right. The content of the communication and the content of the sharing should be basic in the approach to methods of worship, since it forms its origin and purpose.

It is, of course, usually easier to write or talk about what ought to be than to explain exactly how it might become so. At this point we indicate one or two lessons which the early church had to learn which may indicate the way for us. However one views the origin and purpose of the Acts of the Apostles it does seem to be intended to indicate how the Church came to be

[10] *The Gagging of God*, Hodder and Stoughton 1969.

what it did become, and the hints are worthy of our consideration.

They had to learn to be a *mission with a message*. This plainly is not all that they were, as Acts 2:41–7 indicates. But the impression given is of the natural and determined way in which their lives were characterized by the sense of being sent for a purpose. This was not a matter of talking about the gospel all the time. Indeed one striking feature is the way in which it was some outstanding deed or incident which caused the crowds to gather and the opportunity for witness to be given. Yet living as disciples for Christ and speaking as witnesses to Christ seem to have gone naturally together for them. As Harry S. Boer[11] pointed out, there is no record in Acts of disciples giving a word of Jesus to justify their witnessing. The reason for this, he suggests, is that the impulsion to mission came from within, from their own experience of Christ and from the promptings of the Holy Spirit. It seems that the quality of their worship and fellowship on the one hand was matched by the quality of their witness on the other, and that each fed and sustained the other. To put it in more recent jargon, both their 'come' structures and their 'go' structures were operating!

Secondly they had to learn to be *manœuvrable in face of changing circumstances*. This was far from easy for the earliest Christians to learn, being largely, if not entirely, of Jewish origin. Their struggles to understand the fact that the gospel was for Gentiles too is movingly told in the Acts (see the Acts 15 account of the Council of Jerusalem, for example). But they had to learn and the Church grew as they did so, and as they learned the theology which lay behind such a necessity. Indeed at one point Paul seems to declare that this is what the gospel is about! (Eph. 2:11–3:21). And this is important; they were manœuvred by the implications of the gospel and their experience of it. How much of our worship involves us in pondering the relationship between the gospel message and the necessary changes in our structures and activities which it requires?

Next, they had to learn *awareness of the need of others*. Much of the development of the early Church as told in Acts has to do with relieving the needs of those who were will, crippled or poor.

11 *Pentecost and Missions*, Lutterworth 1961.

This was matched by a concern to care for their own under-privileged, too. Again it is not so much for a list of caring activities one pleads as for a sense of being open to need and available to meet it wherever it is found. So often our special efforts and our special preachers seem unrelated to the needs of the people round about because they do not happen to come at the time that particular crises occur. No wonder people do not respond to our invitation, since they do not have the impression that we care for them as people, only as 'pew-fodder'. It is only as the Church in a given area is known to care that others recognize the genuine Christian faith that it professes. Do we allow the area and its needy really to invade the quiet of our worship?

In the fourth place they had to learn what it meant to be a *charismatic community*. They were impelled by the Holy Spirit, discovering and enjoying and using the gifts which He gave, and the abilities which He released. And it was in this way that they discovered that every Christian was necessary to the fellowship as every member to the body. In this way, too, they learned what unity really meant, and were encouraged to preserve it. The pictures we have, however brief, of their worship, give one a sense of freedom, and of variety of gift and participation in worship. By contrast our worship seems somewhat formalized and limited to few leaders and many followers. A discovery of new pattern of charismatic worship may well set us freer along this line. But it must set us free for worship and service in this age. To this we now turn.

Chapter Nine

NOW

IT IS DOUBTFUL whether any age or culture has been as self-conscious about its uniqueness as ours. We are the *technological age*, increasingly harnessing the power and resources of the natural world through advanced scientific knowledge and sophisticated techniques. We are the *global age*, establishing contact, communication and accessibility with remote parts of the world, and now launching further and further into unknown areas of the universe. We belong to the era in which man is spoken of as having *come of age*, enjoying increasing self-reliance, finding more and more explanations within the world of natural phenomena, needing less and less to revert to the 'supernatural' explanations of bye-gone days. We are also an overtly *pluralistic age*, deeply aware of the variety of culture, race, thought-form and religion in the world, and of the right of men to hold to their own views while working alongside one another.

The major difficulty for historians of the future may be to find a single title with which to describe our particular piece of human history. One could go on multiplying possible ways by which they might indicate the supreme characteristic of our time. Fortunately, however, that is not our task here. Yet we cannot leave this consideration without drawing a conclusion in relation to our thoughts on worship. It is that our 'now' is a different 'now' from that of all previous ages. Ours is not the 'now' of Palmerston, Pitt, Henry VIII or Herod. It is therefore not the 'now' of Shaftesbury, Wesley, Luther or Paul. If we are tempted to think this to be a trifling point we might ask ourselves how much of our worship seems to presuppose that we are sharing their 'now' with them.

The pressing question here (often present in modern theological and ecclesiastical debate, even when not specifically mentioned), is that of the continuity and discontinuity of present-day with earlier Christianity. Moreover, since the rate of cultural change seems to be accelerating all the time, so that future generations of Christians will find the question even more acute, we must face up to the problem of the relationship of present-day Christianity to that of the future, too. To put it bluntly, 'Are we of a piece with whichever "good old days" of religion we choose: and are we in fact "building for the future"?'—(the usual defence of youth clubs which break church property and don't attend church!).

The significance of the question can be demonstrated simply by asking which part of worship is *not* influenced by considerations of faithfulness to the past, awareness of the requirements of the present, and sensitivity to the needs of the future. What is the most appropriate shape and construction of a new church? How ought the seats/pews to be arranged, and in relation to one another, or pulpit, or table or entrance? What is suitable dress for worship, either for conducting it or simply participating in it? What type or types of music are fitting or desirable? Which translations of the Bible should be read? Should there be a sermon, or has it lost its value as a proper means of communicating something? Which thought-forms are appropriate for our prayers and preaching, and what kind of vocabulary is acceptable? What shape of liturgy, type of self-expression, kind of atmosphere and ethos are required?

At each of these points, and probably at many more than we realize, our responses to such questions reveal our difficulty in handling our present in relation to our past and our future, corporately and individually. In picture language, do we travel up the river of our worship like oarsmen, moving into the future with our eyes fixed firmly on the past; or like the cox, seeing only what lies ahead; or like passengers on a pleasure steamer facing across the river and so enjoying a series of 'present' views of the river and the bank, each following the other in rapid succession? It is possible in this way grossly to over-simply the problem; it is difficult to over-emphasize it.[1]

As so often happens in considering Christianity, however,

---

[1] For different approaches to 'the problem of faith and history', see Daniel Fuller, *Easter Faith and History*, Tyndale Press 1968; Van A. Harvey, *The Historian and the Believer*, S.C.M. 1967; and Alan Richardson, *History, Sacred and Profane*, S.C.M. 1964.

the presence of apparently insurmountable obstacles may well indicate the way to the truest view. But we find the truth, not by jettisoning one or more of the possibilities, but by seeking to hold them all in a proper tension. In the theological realm we have only to ask about the nature of God, or the person of Jesus Christ, or the operation of the Holy Spirit, or even whether salvation is present or future, to indicate our line of thought here. In each case it is easier to find a simple solution by dropping one or more of the possible answers. But our Christian traditions have wisely sought to safeguard the variety of well-grounded answers as vital parts of the total, if complex, answer to each question. We often have to choose between a manageable but inadequate simplification and a series of statements or insights, each authentic in itself, each commanding one's assent, each on 'our' side of the boundary of understanding. When all are put together, however, they seem no longer to be under our control, but point us beyond the boundaries of our total understanding. In doing so they point us to a reality greater than ourselves, which we can affirm but never control. Rather it asks of me a submission to its control by a commitment which takes me beyond complete understanding but deeper into reality.

The question of past, present and future in relation to worship is a question of this kind; the problem posed by my 'now' in relation to that of my forefathers and my descendants. I can try to 'live in the past', or to 'affirm the present', or even to 'build for the future'. Each has an enticing simplicity about it, which explains why each is in some ways so readily and effectively defensible. Yet each is in fact an impossibility, an illusion. The past is no longer available as an ethos for our existence. The future is too elusive and unprogrammed to lend total meaning to what we do now. And the present without past or future is as unintelligible a concept as a stretch of river without source or destination. Our worship, like our Christianity as a whole, must somehow celebrate our past without becoming locked up in it, affirm our present without being constrained by it; and anticipate our future without being beguiled by it.

Nor is this problem a particularly new one in type (though its degree and intensity may be greater than ever before, because

of the speed of change we experience and the variety of life as
we know it). Every human being and community lives with
this problem every day. Every Christian individual and
community faces the Christian manifestation of it.[2] From the
Israelites in the wilderness, with Egypt behind and the promised
land ahead; through the early Christians with their Jewish
background behind them and the spread of the Church among
the Gentiles ahead; to the present-day Church with her various
traditions behind her and the challenge of unity, service and
witness ahead, the problem of the relationship between past,
present and future has been a perennial one.

We may go further and observe that the biblical writers
were themselves aware of the problem, and that they offer us
some pointers towards a solution. We begin with the Old
Testament prophets. At one time it was a matter of debate
whether the prophetic task was to 'foretell' or to 'forth-tell'.
The debate was popularly settled in favour of the latter, though
not to the total exclusion of the former. One can approach
this question from a slightly different angle, however, by
asking, not 'Did they foretell or forthtell?' but 'By what criteria
did they do either?'. One major criterion was the known
character of God. In the light of their insight into who He was,
known by His declared purposes and deeds in their previous
history, the prophets described both how He judged the present
situation and how He could be expected to act in relation to it.
At this point foretelling and forthtelling share some common
ground. The prophets were in no sense freed from awareness of
the details of the present situation, nor from taking a common-
sense view of possible eventualities in the future. But they
resolutely refused to be governed by either or both. In the light
of the revealed character of God they harangued, invited,
commanded or comforted their fellows, seeking an appropriate
present and future response to the God who had already
declared Himself in the past and had promised to be faithful
to them in the present and the future. Celebration of the past,
affirmation of the present and anticipation of the future are all
component parts of the prophet's message, whether optimistic
or pessimistic at each level.

[2] T. S. Garrett, *Christian Worship: An Introductory Outline*, Oxford University
Press 1961, pp. 8ff.

A similar combination is observable in the Psalms. Personalized and autobiographical though many of them are in form, they still lean heavily in their devotion upon the great moments in their past. Creation, Exodus, Promised Land, Monarchy recur not just as historical events but as activities of the living God, activities which the Psalmist lives through again in the present. In the strength of such assurances about the character, faithfulness and power of God the Psalmist can affirm even an uncertain present and look forward to an unknown but hopeful future.

In the New Testament a similar kind of pattern emerges, seen most clearly in its focus upon Jesus Christ Himself. Thus we read of 'Jesus Christ yesterday and today the same, and for ever' (Heb. 13:8, literal trans.). The comprehensiveness of such christology is exhibited by stress upon Christ as the Word who was 'in the beginning with God' (John 1:2), as the Son 'through whom also he (God) created the world' (Heb. 1:2) and as 'the image of the invisible God', in whom 'all things were created' (Col. 1:16). The 'present' Christ has a long and meaningful past. In the same way His existence and significance are projected into the future, too. He is described as claiming the final place in judgement ('On that day many will say to me "Lord, Lord" '—Matt. 7:22). He is referred to as 'heir of all things', by God's appointment (Heb. 1:2); it is declared that 'we must all appear before the judgment seat of Christ' (II Cor. 5:10). More positively, we read of 'a plan for the fullness of time, to unite all things in him' (Eph. 1:10).

The importance of this material lies not only in its precise content, but also in the relationship of each part to the whole story of Christ. Thus the significance of the earthly life of Christ can be seen as the (pre-existent) Word made flesh (John 1:14), as the revealing of the 'first-born of all creation' (Col. 1:15). In other words the value of the life of Christ lies not only in what He did but also in who He was; the present is filled with some of its meaning from the past. In the same way the significance of His earthly ministry is projected into the future, as suggested above. Parts of the earthly ministry of Christ cannot properly be understood except in relation to its significance for the future. So we find ourselves back at Hebrews 13:8, affirming that each part of Christ's existence must be affirmed for a full understanding of the meaning of the whole: past, present and future.

And it is so for the life of the Church. The early Christians declared their message in terms of their past (initially their Jewish heritage fulfilled and exploded by Jesus Christ) and what God had done in it; their present (in terms of their daily experience of the presence of Christ, to which they witnessed in word and deed) and what God was continuing to do; and their future (in terms of fellowship, mission and consummation) and what God would do. Their evangelistic message, their community life and their individual life-style were all based upon this three-dimensional outlook.

All of this involves an action which is physically impossible in the literal sense—tri-focalization. (Even bi-focal spectacles enable the wearer to focus upon one or other distance, not both at once.) But the Christian outlook on life is and must remain tri-focal. If he jettisons his history the present becomes distorted. If he neglects the present—in the interests of past or future—life becomes unrealistic and illusory. If he ignores the future, then history takes on a cyclical rather than a linear aspect[3] and concepts of growth, hope, purpose lose much of their meaning. What is more, all of this is not only unhelpful pragmatically, it is also unnecessary for the Christian, since the God whom he worships both comprehends and transcends all time—past, present and future. It was partly to express the closeness of Jesus to God the Father that the New Testament writers describe Him in terms of past, present and future. All three find their single 'being' in God, whose undivided 'now' is eternal. It is only for us that time is actually past, present and future; for God everything simply 'is'.

The implications of such considerations for our worship today have already been touched upon in a narrow sense in the chapter on sacraments (Ch. 7). Here we may extend that consideration to apply to all our worship.

First, if we are properly to relate to our past then there must be adequate time in worship for recollection. One of the significant features about Christianity is its rootage in history; its relation to and dependence upon a particular life, in a

---

[3] H. S. Crossley, 'The Universality of the Gospel', in John Stacey (ed.), *About the Gospel*, Methodist Local Preachers' Department 1971, pp. 94ff.

specific setting at a precise time. And there is its continued link with that life, both through the operation of the Holy Spirit in the world and through the ongoing life of the Church. Does our worship show sufficient reliance upon that foundation (I Cor. 3:11), not simply as a starting point (since one has to begin somewhere) but as a normative factor in all Christian worship and living?

We may press this question in a number of ways.[4] Does our preaching devote enough time to the telling of the 'foundation stories' of the Christian Church, or do we assume that everyone knows? And are these stories looked at in terms of their present significance, or is that looked upon as an impossible task? When Christian love is our theme in worship, how much sense is there of being obedient to the pattern of love revealed in Christ? Would a regular visitor to our services become aware of the whole picture of Christ revealed in the New Testament, or only of certain selected aspects which fit in with our churchmanship, theology or present setting?

Another way of approaching this strand in our worship—the necessity of recollection—is to enquire about the sense of depending basically upon what God has done in history rather than upon our current religious temperature. An enormous load is lifted from the shoulders of Christians who realize that the validity of the faith does not depend upon their being able to summon up sufficient zeal, excitement or even conviction in order to 'make the thing go'! Primarily the Christian faith depends upon what God has already done in Christ, and we are properly tied to that. Paul's warning and advice fits in here: 'no other foundation can be laid than that which is laid, which is Jesus Christ.' It is a warning against building anywhere else: it is encouraging advice because we don't need to build anywhere else. Does our worship echo such assurance?

Secondly, if we are to relate properly to the future then there must be room in our worship for anticipation, too. This means that we take seriously the description of Christians as 'pilgrim people'. This needs to be given full weight in relation to the changes through which the world passes. The writer to the Hebrews really asserts that God made the world to pass through

---

[4] The basic material for the next two paragraphs is contained in Ch. 2.

these changes ('through whom he (God) made the ages' would be a literal translation of Hebrews 1:2). This is not to say that all change will of necessity be beneficial: but it is to deny that change of itself should be resisted or treated as unfortunate. The living God also moves through the changes. Too often He has to leave His 'pilgrim people' behind. Our worship should from time to time enable us to face the fact of change. It should also aid us as we seek together to discern how God's will is being worked out among the changes of our modern world. What are the 'signs' of His presence? Where can His people co-operate in this task? What hinders God's Kingdom from being established amongst us within our own culture?

Our looking to the future should have another effect upon our worship. It should remind us of the limitations and partiality of everything we say or do in our services. As Paul puts it, 'our knowledge and our prophecy alike are partial' (I Cor. 13:9 N.E.B.). This is not to undervalue what we know and have experienced of the gospel. It is not to suggest that God has left us without sufficient light by which to walk the pilgrim way. But it is to remind ourselves that there is always new light to be enjoyed, new depths of truth to be explored, new experiences to be entered into. By contrast our human tendency is to find security by being totally satisfied with the present state of our insight, understanding, discipleship, systematization. The result of this is fossilization which allows neither life nor movement. John Stott has argued that the Christian gospel must be old, and is getting older every day, but that it must also be 'freshly understood ... freshly applied ... freshly experienced'.[5] Our worship should enable us to hold together the oldness and the newness of the faith. We do not in this way undermine our past; but we do realize its implications for the future which opens out before us.

A third implication of worshipping with anticipation is the hope that things will not always be as they are now. Harvey Cox speaks of this aspect in terms of the fantasy of Christian worship.[6] By this he means that Christians dare to meet together and picture a world in which demonic powers do not have such great influence, and where love, kindness, justice and peace are

[5] *Christ the Controversialist*, pp. 38–9.
[6] *The Feast of Fools*, Harper and Row 1969.

acknowledged by all. Faber develops the thought[7] (in harmony with the theme in Cox), of the Christian minister (in the hospital ward, for example), as the court jester of the piece. It was the task of the jester, by his merry quips, not simply to entertain but also to cut everyone down to size, including occasionally the monarch himself. Faber argues that the perspective which the Christian minister in the hospital brings to life has the effect of cutting everyone and everything else down to proper proportions. So the Christian, we may go on to affirm, as he worships Almighty God, begins to see everyone and everything else in proper perspective. There are numerous biblical examples of this principle. All earthly power and power holders; all changes and causes of change; all threats and originators of threat are seen in true perspective when focused in the presence of God. Authoritarian regimes are right to see Christianity as a threat to their continuance. It is so precisely because it sees them in their true light and size. Martin Luther's hymn *Ein' feste Burg* ('A safe strong-hold') puts this point with great clarity.

We are surely right therefore to expect our hope to be renewed in worship. This is not the same as being encouraged to sit back and wait for God to bring in His kingdom. It is precisely the opposite of this, for biblical hope is active in bringing about that which God encourages it to hope for. To hope in this way for God's Kingdom is to commit oneself to work for it; indeed it is to risk all one's life on it. Hopeful worship produces constructive action.

Worship related to the future, worship with anticipation as we have termed it, has one other ingredient. It casts out fear. Paul again sums this up in one of the most majestic collections of thoughts and words in the New Testament, Romans 8:31–9. Here we see the bringing together of past and future (in harmony with the argument of this chapter) very clearly illustrated. Because of what God has done for us in Christ, Paul argues, and because of its implications, we may be sure that nothing in the future will separate us from His love in Christ. As we might transpose it, 'neither pollution nor nuclear war, soil erosion nor sea poisoning, biological weapons nor nerve gases' shall be able to separate us from God's love in

[7] *Pastoral Care in the Modern Hospital*, S.C.M. 1971.

6

Christ. Rather than preventing us from working against such entities in our world, such a confidence enables us properly to oppose them and do something about them, properly because we no longer act in panic and fear, but out of a calm assurance that we are in God's will and can remain so.

Thirdly we must ask about the effect of all these things upon our present experience of worship, and our proper affirmation of the present. Here we enter into realms best described by the word 'peace'. It has various recognizable characteristics.[8]

It is, for example, trustful. There is a calm unshakeable quality about it because it knows that everything is safe in God's hands. It is an inner quality resting upon a conviction about and reliance upon the character of God Himself. It is neither frenetic nor frenzied, despairing nor despondent. This inner repose needs renewal as we contemplate who God is. Our worship should provide opportunity both for contemplation which deepens our peace and for ways of expressing it together.

Peace also bears itself patiently. Seeing the world as in God's hands, it recognizes that history takes time to make, partly because of the slowness of men to recognize or do God's will, and partly because of the genuine freedom God has given man to resist Him if he so wishes.

But it is also active. Patient it may be, but lazy it may never be. For it perceives God's purposes, and feels every failure to achieve them as an insult to God Himself. What to others may be viewed as disgraceful or unfortunate may for the Christian be blasphemous. He cannot view the world with complacency. If change is slow then all the more reason for making one's contribution mightily.

And it is joyful. The source of joy is not the world alone, for so much here will rob us of our joy, and will be a cause of end-less fluctuation. The source of the Christian's joy is God Himself. 'Rejoice in the Lord' (Phil. 4:4) is Paul's advice: not 'Rejoice in your circumstances'.

Finally it is a communal experience. God's gift of peace is not meant to be kept to oneself; nor will it allow its possessor to keep to himself. For it is part of the total peace which God

---

[8] J. G. Davies, *Worship and Mission*, p. 130. 'This word indicates all aspects of human life in its full and God-given maturity: righteousness, trust, fellowship, peace etc. This simple word summarizes all the gifts of the messianic age.'

offers to all men. The experience of peace will constantly make us more aware of the world around us and God's purposes for it.

Trifocalization may be physically impossible, but it is spiritually invigorating. It gives a Christian that largeness of view which is more worthy of the greatness of the God he worships. It gives proper place to God's initiative in history, and its faith is based on that. It enables a view into the future which is neither shallowly optimistic nor hopelessly pessimistic. It provides for peace in the present which is both calm and active, trusting and striving for God's will to be done on earth. It spans the whole range of our knowledge of God's activities. It enables us to celebrate our Christian past, to anticipate our Christian future and to affirm our Christian present. In it all we see the results of man's rebellion: but we risk our lives on God's sovereignty and the victory of His love, declared in Christ and to be consummated at the end. We dare to believe that such worship *can* be 'momentous', 'urgent' and 'glorious'.

ONE WAY of concluding the writing of a book is to ask oneself what one hopes will be its effect on those who will read it. In terms of this book what is it that one covets for regular and faithful worshippers, Sunday by Sunday, in the life of our churches of all denominations?

First, that worship as a habit may not be only a matter of habit. It is too late in this book to enter into any debate about the value of 'habitual' activities, except to observe that for most of us the 'habitual' elements of life form the necessary core of our existence. But this is different from habitual activity which, because habitual, loses meaning or ceases to have any exhilaration or anticipation associated with it. In a way the major question is not whether the noun 'habit' ought to be ascribed to worship, but which adjectives, if any, one attaches to the noun. One's hope is that through the consideration of presuppositions of worship there may come a greater degree of expectancy; expectancy that worship may become more meaningful because more firmly linked to the realities which lie at the heart of the Christian faith; expectancy that our worship may be spiritual and true because it is based upon a greater understanding of God and His ways with us, and upon a deeper response on our part to His claims upon our lives.

Secondly, one looks for a greater degree of questioning of the contents of our worship. What is the value of the particular ordering of worship to which we are accustomed? Which basic realities about God, man, salvation, Church, world, life are they meant to be expressing, or offering or illuminating? How far do the things we do, say, observe and share in worship actually give expression to our state of faith, grace and response? How far do they lead us on in that state? Does worship enable me to enter more fully into the truth of things?

Next one hopes for a development of the awareness—already growing among Christians—that worship at set times and in set places and forms must not be dissociated from life as a whole, since it is in fact part of that life. How far does our

Sunday worship respond to the stimulus of life through the week? What kind of tension exists between the two—a healthy or unhealthy one? Can I bring into worship the successes and the failures of my personal life, the pressures and the comforts of family, the grinding boredom or the absorbing interest of work, the exciting achievements and the degrading scandals of the world at large? Does it seem appropriate, and is it made possible, for me to offer that which lies at the heart of all the contrasts outlined above, namely a fairly ordinary life? Do I feel myself to be myself in worship? And do I experience the oneness of belonging with others to the Body of Christ? Is there a living relationship between worship and living, not because I keep them in watertight compartments of life, joined only because I must proceed from one to the other and back again in the cycle of life, nor because I seek to make the one as much like the other as possible, but because I perceive by faith the presence of the same God in both, and by the insights of faith can make sense of both by the same frame of reference— His purposes for the creation He has redeemed through Christ and is active in by the Holy Spirit?

Fourthly, one could wish that there might be an enlarged apprehension of the fact that worship cannot safely be separated from theology either, or at least from the continuing attempt to be clear about the content of our faith and about its relationship to life as a whole. This is not to appeal for elitist congregations consisting only of the intellectuals. Christian theological under-standing suffers when it is limited to that level. But it is to encourage every believer to seek for a greater clarity about what he believes, a firmer grasp of the reasons for so believing, and a growing awareness of the implications of that belief for his participation in worship.

In the fifth place, and arising out of the above, there is the need for churches to recognize that instruction in the Christian faith—using the word 'instruction' in the widest sense—should be a constant part of the life of every local church if its worship is to grow and deepen—in spirit and in truth. In the end it is this double test applied by our Lord which is most important. But if our worship is to be 'in spirit and in truth' then we need to be helped to grow in our inner experience of the faith and our apprehension of the truth. And this is a continuing task, not only because new people should constantly be joining the ranks, but also because for all of us there is always more to be experienced and learned. Worship properly plays a part in this deepening process; it also expresses it and is enriched by it as we seek the goal with which we began, that *our* worship might be 'the most momentous, the most urgent, the most glorious action that can take place in human life', and that God may be experienced in worship at the centre of His people, not relegated to the gallery.

INTRODUCTION

1 What do we mean by 'Christian worship'?

2 Is it helpful to speak of the 'major components' of Christian worship, and if so, what are they?

3 Which acts of worship have been most meaningful for you during the past six months, and why?

4 Does the worship you are accustomed to share in need more form or more freedom? Could it possibly combine more of both? If so, how?

CHAPTER ONE

1 In what ways do you find it most meaningful to think or talk about God? How do these ways influence your worship?

2 How could the content of our worship enable us to think more clearly about God and experience His presence more deeply?

3 What do you consider to be the proper relationship between acts of worship and everyday life?

4 Prepare an order of service and an outline sermon, based upon consideration of one of the attributes of God.

CHAPTER TWO

1 How far, and in what ways, does the worship you share in express the historical rootage of the Christian faith? Are there other or more effective ways in which it might do so?

2 What do we mean by 'a *personal* knowledge of God through Jesus Christ'? Does the worship you share in make you aware of the presence of God? If so, how?

3 How legitimate is it to use the overall pattern of Jesus' earthly ministry as a guide to the shape of our worship? If we do so, what reflections upon our current orders of service are prompted by this approach?

4 Prepare an order of service and an outline sermon, on the theme 'Emmanuel . . . God with us' (Matt. 1:23).

CHAPTER THREE

1 Passages like John 16:14, 'He will glorify me, for he will take what is mine and declare it unto you', raise the question of the reality of Jesus to present-day believers. How is that reality experienced and evidenced?

2 John also records words about the Holy Spirit 'convincing of sin' (John 16:8–11). How is this to be understood, and how far and in what ways ought this to happen in worship? Can those who lead worship appropriately prepare for this aspect?

3 The Holy Spirit is said to give understanding to the believer, as in I Corinthians 2:6–13. What implications does this have for worship? What kind of knowledge is imparted? Why is the Spirit necessary?

4 Prepare an order of service, and an outline sermon, on some aspect of the work of the Holy Spirit.

CHAPTER FOUR

1 How far does worship welcome, reveal, affirm, condemn, restore, challenge, transform, inform, fulfil you? What other

verbs would you add, or which would you wish to remove, if any?

2 Is it possible to affirm both modern man's 'coming of age' and his dependence upon God? If so, how is this affirmation made and explored in our worship?

3 Does worship as you experience it draw upon the resources of your whole personality, or is there imbalance in its appeal and influence?

4 Prepare an order of service and an outline sermon, on the theme of Romans 12:1.

CHAPTER FIVE

1 How can the sense of 'oneness' in the local congregation be improved in worship and outside it?

2 What are the respective roles of the ordained minister and the layman in the church, and how ought these to be expressed in worship?

3 What are the meeting points between set liturgical orders and spontaneous approaches to worship? Can the two be combined in a single service, and if so, how?

4 Prepare an order of service and sermon outline, on the subject of the nature and life of the Church.

CHAPTER SIX

1 In what ways should (a) the types of worship discernible in the New Testament, and (b) the developed traditions of worship over the centuries influence the form and content of our worship today?

2 Should the Bible be the only book from which the 'lessons'

are read in worship, or on which sermons are based? Which criteria do you use when answering such a question?

3   How far, and in what ways is the message of the Bible relevant today?

4   Prepare an order of service and sermon outline for Bible Sunday.

CHAPTER SEVEN

1   How would you explain the relationship between God's saving activity in Christ as recounted in the gospels and our sacramental experience today?

2   What do you understand by 'the presence of Christ' in the Lord's Supper?

3   How do concepts of past, present and future influence our approach to the sacraments?

4   Prepare outlines of two talks to a class preparing for membership of the church, or confirmation; one on baptism, the other on the Lord's Supper.

CHAPTER EIGHT

1   How do you expect worship in church to be related to life in the world?

2   Should worship involve consideration of major questions facing the contemporary world? If so, how can this be done?

3   How do the evangelistic and social concerns of the christian Church relate to one another, and how can this relationship be celebrated and experienced in worship, then expressed in daily life?

4 Prepare an order of service and sermon outline, using one major contemporary concern as its basis.

CHAPTER NINE

1 Does the past, the present or the future figure most highly in your preparation for and participation in worship? How ought the three to be related?

2 How would you define 'christian hope' in the contemporary world? How is it celebrated in worship?

3 In what ways ought our worship to enable us to discern the signs of God's presence in the contemporary world?

4 Prepare an order of service and an outline sermon on 'History and Faith'.